Consultant

M. Chinery B.A.

Editor

A. Sheehan B.A.

Illustrators

John Barber
Bernard Robinson
Pat Lenander
Sean Milne
Brian Pearce
John Marriott
Tony Herbert

Production

Jean Nimmo

SBN 361 021038
© Macdonald & Co Ltd 1972

Printed in Great Britain by
Hazell Watson & Viney Ltd
Aylesbury, Bucks

PURNELL'S
DISCOVERING
NATURE

PURNELL'S DISCOVERING NATURE

Angela Sheehan

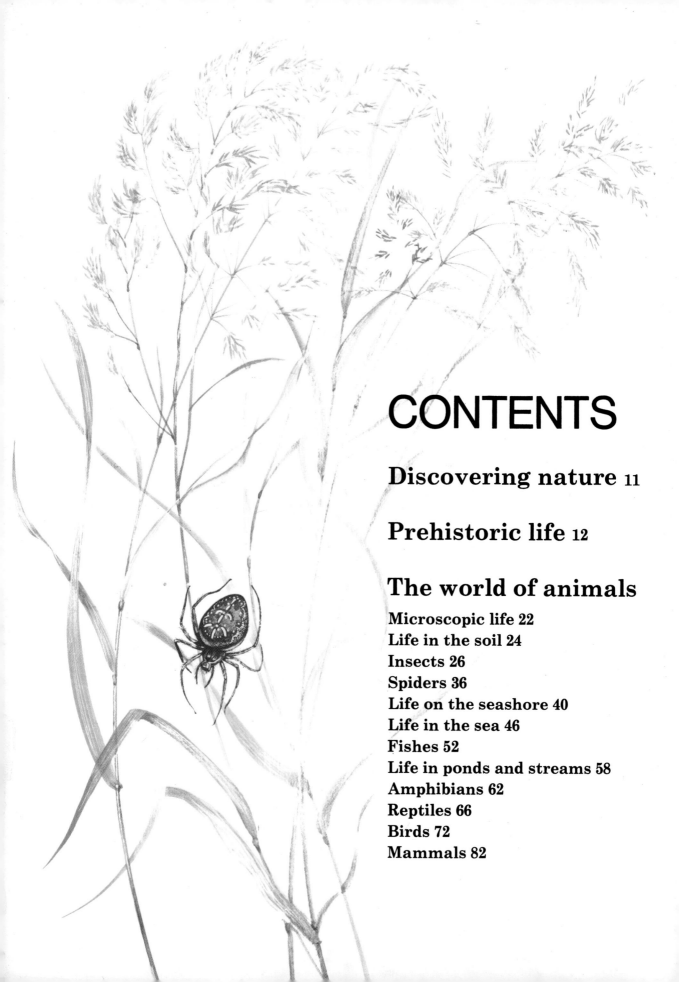

CONTENTS

Discovering nature 11

Prehistoric life 12

The world of animals

Discovering Nature

During the summer you often see bees and other insects buzzing from flower to flower. They are feeding on the nectar. The bees drink the nectar and gather pollen to take home to their young. They do not know that, by carrying pollen from flower to flower, they are helping the flowers to make new seeds.

Without the insects, new flowers could not grow each year and without the flowers the insects would have no food. This is just one of the many ways in which animals and plants depend upon each other. There are millions of different plants and animals. In this book you can read about many of them and discover how they live.

Prehistoric Life

Prehistoric animals lived on Earth long before there were people to write about them. We know about prehistoric animals because their bones sometimes sank in the mud and were turned to stone. These bones can now be found in rocks. They are called fossils.

When the fossil bones of a large prehistoric animal are found, the rock is carefully chipped away from the bones. Then the bones are put together so that people can see what the skeleton of the animal looked like. Sometimes animals are preserved almost intact.

Fossil skeleton of Iguanodon

Insect preserved in amber

Footprint of dinosaur

Ichthyosaur fossil

Ammonite fossil

Strange fossils

Insects have been found trapped in gum which dripped from pine trees millions of years ago. As the sticky gum slowly hardened to amber the outline of the insect left its shape perfectly.

Strange fossils are the tracks left by prehistoric animals in mud. When the mud hardened to rock the footprints were preserved. Today they are sometimes found in rock quarries.

Many fossils are the skeletons and shells of animals which lived in the sea. Some rocks are made up almost entirely of these fossils.

Fossil graptolites. These strange little animals lived in tubes of many shapes stuck to rocks under the sea

Life begins in the sea

The first plants and animals lived in the sea. They would have been too small to be seen without a microscope. Slowly more and more animals appeared. Jellyfish floated in the clear water, worms burrowed in the mud, and trilobites crawled over the sea-bed looking for food.

Most trilobites had no eyes. They used feelers to find their way about. When a trilobite was frightened it could curl up into a ball. Trilobites were the largest of the early animals. But few were longer than your thumb.

One of the oldest fossils is the imprint of a worm and a jellyfish in rock

Life in the sea 600 million years ago

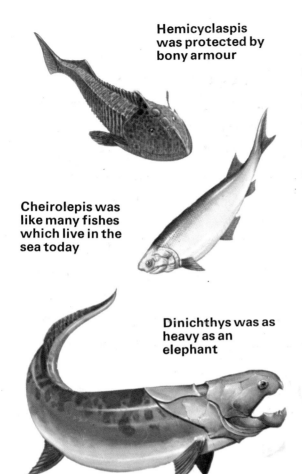

Hemicyclaspis was protected by bony armour

Cheirolepis was like many fishes which live in the sea today

Dinichthys was as heavy as an elephant

Fishes

The first fishes had no jaws. Their bodies were covered with bony plates which protected them like a suit of armour. The first fishes with jaws were called placoderms. Most of them were small, but one was 30 feet long and as heavy as an elephant. It was the biggest creature in the world at that time.

As time passed by, other fishes appeared in the sea. Some had bony skeletons like most fish alive today. Others were much like modern sharks. All the bones in their bodies were soft.

Amphibians

Many millions of years ago the climate of the world became very dry. Less and less rain fell. Big rivers turned into muddy pools and many fishes died. But some bony fishes could breathe out of the water. They also had strong fins which they could use as legs. Some of these fishes crawled out of the water and began to live on the land.

The fishes living on the land slowly changed. Their legs grew stronger. Their tails grew longer. Their heads grew big and bony. These were the first amphibians. Amphibians are animals which spend most of their time on land. But they usually go back to the water to lay their eggs.

Some early amphibians grew very large. One was as long as a crocodile with a heavy body and short, fat legs.

Miobatrachus looked rather like a frog

Early amphibian

Mesosaurus, a
sea-dwelling
reptile

Triassochelys, an
ancestor of
tortoises

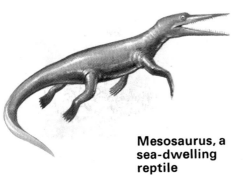

Hypsognathus
had bony spikes
on its head

Reptiles

After millions of years some amphibians began
to change. They grew scales on their bodies and
laid eggs with hard shells. There was no need to
lay these eggs in the water. They could be laid
on land. These animals were the first reptiles.

The reptiles were so successful that more and
more different kinds appeared. And not all of
them lived on land. Some reptiles took to the air.
Others went back to the sea.

Stegosaurus

Dinosaurs

The biggest reptiles were the dinosaurs. The word dinosaur means terrible lizard. But most of the dinosaurs were harmless plant-eaters. One of these was Stegosaurus. It had bony flaps on its back and big spikes on its tail. When Stegosaurus was attacked it swung its spiked tail like a club.

Brontosaurus was one of the biggest dinosaurs. Fossils show that it must have been over 70 feet long. Brontosaurus was so heavy that it probably could not stand for long on the land. It spent most of its time in lakes where the water helped to support its huge body. Brontosaurus needed so much food that it ate plants all day long.

Dinosaurs were not intelligent animals. The very biggest of them had a brain the size of a chicken's egg.

Hylonomus, one of the earliest reptiles, was the size of a lizard

Brontosaurus

Tyrannosaurus

The enemies of the peaceful plant-eating dinosaurs were the meat-eaters. The largest meat-eating dinosaur was the terrible Tyrannosaurus. This dinosaur stood 20 feet tall on its powerful back legs. Its front legs were very small but they had sharp claws for gripping animals. Tyrannosaurus had a large head with huge jaws and long sharp teeth. Some animals could run fast enough to escape Tyrannosaurus. Others, like Triceratops, had bony armour to protect them.

Dinosaurs ruled the world for many millions of years. Then they all became extinct. No one knows why this happened. Perhaps the climates of the world became too dry and there was not enough food for such large animals.

Archaeopteryx is the earliest known bird. It had claws on its wings and teeth in its beak. We know what it looked like from its fossil

Triceratops

The first bird

While the great dinosaurs ruled the land the first bird with feathers flew in the air. It is called Archaeopteryx. A fossil has been found which shows just how this bird must have looked.

Archaeopteryx was the size of a crow. It had feathers on its wings like the birds living today. But it had teeth in its beak like the flying reptiles which lived at the time. Archaeopteryx had weak wings and could not fly very well. It probably fluttered from tree to tree.

Tyrannosaurus

Early mammals

While the great dinosaurs were alive there were small furry animals running about. They were so small that the huge meat-eating dinosaurs did not notice them. These animals were the first mammals. They looked like rats and they ate reptile eggs and insects.

When the dinosaurs became extinct the mammals grew larger. There were sloths as big as trees and pigs as big as donkeys.

Modern mammals

Many of the early mammals became extinct and others took their place. Slowly all of the modern mammals appeared. But some of the early mammals survived in places which were cut off by sea from the rest of the world. Some of them are still alive today in Australia and South America. There are mammals which rear their young in pouches on their bodies. And there are strange mammals which lay eggs.

Today mammals are the most important animals in the world. One of them is man.

The sloth Megatherium compared in size to a man

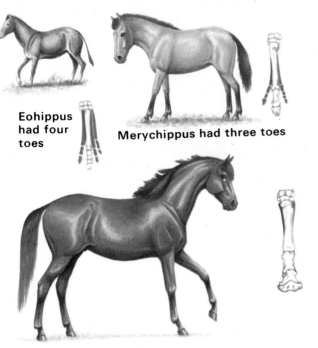

Eohippus had four toes

Merychippus had three toes

The modern horse has one toe

How the horse lost its toes

Fossils show how modern animals have changed over millions of years. The first horse was the size of a fox terrier. It had four toes on its front feet and three toes on its back feet. Millions of years later, horses had three toes on each foot, but the middle toe was the largest. Today horses have just one big toe on each foot. It is called a hoof.

The woolly mammoth

About one million years ago the climates of the world grew cold and many northern lands were covered in ice. This was the Great Ice Age. Only animals like the mammoth were able to live in the snow. The mammoth had a thick woolly coat to keep it warm. Other animals moved south to warmer lands and many never came back.

Woolly mammoth

Sabre-toothed tiger

The sabre-toothed tiger

The sabre-toothed tiger was the greatest enemy of early man. It had teeth as long as daggers. But men were more clever. They killed the sabre-toothed tigers with spears.

Microscopic Life

Some plants and animals are so small that you can only see them with a microscope. Like all living things they are made of cells. The biggest animals and plants are made of millions and millions of cells. Each cell has its own special work to do.

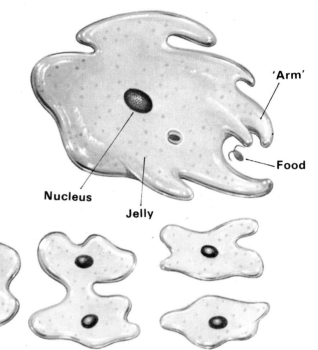

'Arm'

Food

Nucleus

Jelly

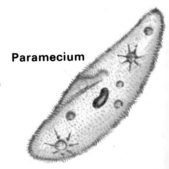

Amoeba splitting in two

The smallest plants and animals have only one cell. Their one cell has to do everything that millions of cells do in bigger plants and animals.

Amoeba

The amoeba is an animal with only one cell. It is a small blob of jelly with a black dot in the middle. This dot is called the nucleus. It is the amoeba's brain.

The amoeba got its name because it is always changing its shape. 'Amoeba' means 'change' in Greek. The amoeba changes its shape so that it can move about. It swims in water by pushing out 'arms' of jelly. As it swims it puts out 'arms' to catch tiny plants for its food.

As it takes in food the tiny amoeba grows. Soon its nucleus splits in two. Then the whole cell splits and there are two amoebae instead of one.

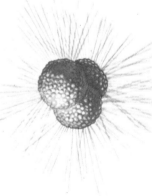

Globigerina

Paramecium

Microscopic plants

Many plants have only one cell. Most of them live in water. They do not catch food like the animals. They make their own food with the same green stuff that is in the leaves of bigger plants. The tiny plants swim near the top of the water because they cannot make food without sunlight.

Spirogyra is a string of cells but each one has its own nucleus and makes its own food. If you look closely at the green scum on top of a pond you will see masses of spirogyra's threads.

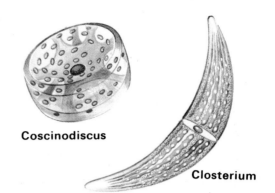

Coscinodiscus

Closterium

These plants have only one cell

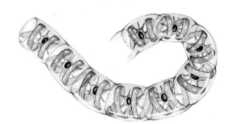

Spirogyra is a chain of cells

Plants or animals?

Some microscopic plants and animals are so alike that scientists cannot tell which they are. Euglena sometimes acts like a plant and sometimes like an animal. If it is green it makes its own food, if not, it catches its food.

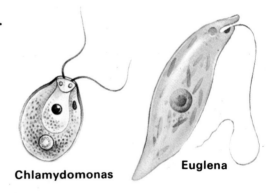

Chlamydomonas

Euglena

These are two 'plant-animals'

Bacteria and viruses

These are the smallest living things. Some bacteria cause diseases but most of them are very useful. Viruses live in the cells of animals and plants. They cause many diseases.

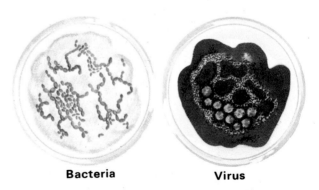

Bacteria

Virus

Bacteria and viruses are the smallest living things. These have been magnified thousands of times

Life in the Soil

If you turn over any stone in your garden or lift one spade of soil, you will probably see at least one animal. You may only see one animal, but there will be many more that you don't see. Thousands of plants and animals live in and on the soil.

The tiniest plants in the soil are the bacteria. These are so small that you cannot see them without a microscope. They are eaten by many animals in the soil.

Many animals make their homes in the soil. There are all sorts of worms and spiders, beetles, centipedes, millipedes, ants and aphids. There are also slugs and snails and woodlice.

Worms

The earthworm has many tiny bristles on its body which help it to tunnel through the earth. As it tunnels it swallows soil. This gives it food as well as more room in which to move. It crushes the soil and absorbs the tiny plants and animals which are in it. Then the rest of the soil passes out of the other end of the worm. The little coils of soil left by the worms are called worm casts.

Without worms the soil would be very hard. Earthworms break up the soil so there is plenty of air and water for the plants.

Slugs and snails

Slugs and snails have soft, slimy bodies. Snails can curl up in their shells when they are in danger. Slugs have no hard shells. They hide during the day so that the sun does not dry them up. Slugs and snails do a lot of damage in gardens because they feed on growing plants.

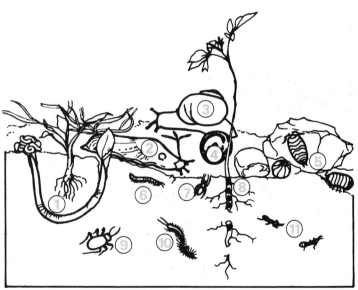

1. Earthworm
2. Round-back slug
3. Roman snail
4. Banded snail
5. Woodlice
6. Millipede
7. Field spider
8. Root aphids
9. Ground beetle
10. Centipede
11. Ants

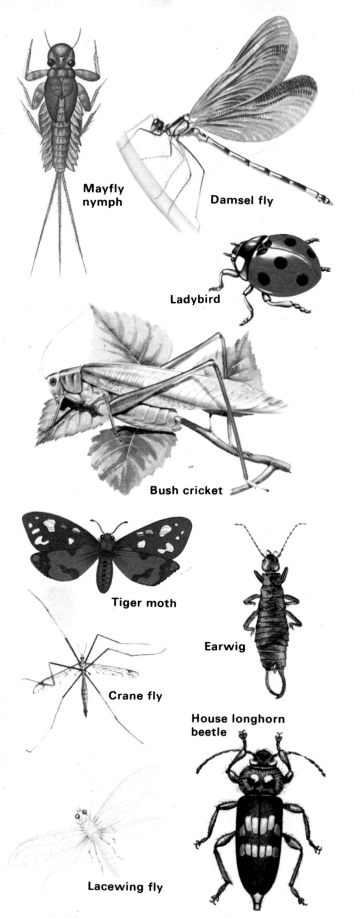

Mayfly nymph

Damsel fly

Ladybird

Bush cricket

Tiger moth

Earwig

Crane fly

House longhorn beetle

Lacewing fly

Insects

Nobody knows just how many kinds of insects there are. Over a million different kinds have been found and more are discovered every day. There are more kinds of insects than all other animals added together.

The insect body

If you look closely at an insect, you will see that its body has three parts. These are the head, the thorax and the abdomen. The body has a hard outer casing, like a suit of armour. It has joints so that the animal can move easily. All insects have six legs. Most of them also have two pairs of wings and two feelers on their heads.

How insects grow up

Most insects lay eggs. Sometimes the young insects which hatch from the eggs look just like their parents. They are called nymphs. But often the young insects look quite different. A caterpillar does not look much like a butterfly but one day it will be one.

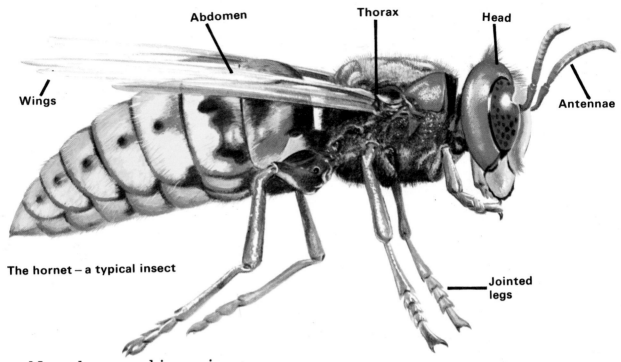

Wings
Abdomen
Thorax
Head
Antennae
Jointed legs

The hornet – a typical insect

Nymphs grow bigger in simple stages. Their hard skins do not grow with them, so they have to be changed. When the skin is too tight the insect takes a short rest. Then it puffs itself up until its skin splits. A new, larger skin has already grown underneath, so the insect just crawls away and leaves the old skin behind. This is called moulting.

Some insects go through four different stages. The egg hatches into a larva, or grub. The larva grows and turns into a pupa. The pupa has a hard skin like a case. Inside this case the insect's body changes. When it has changed the pupa skin splits and out comes the adult insect.

The silverfish nymph moults several times before it is fully grown

The life story of the house fly

Eggs

Larvae

Pupa

Adult fly

Case splits

The life story of a butterfly

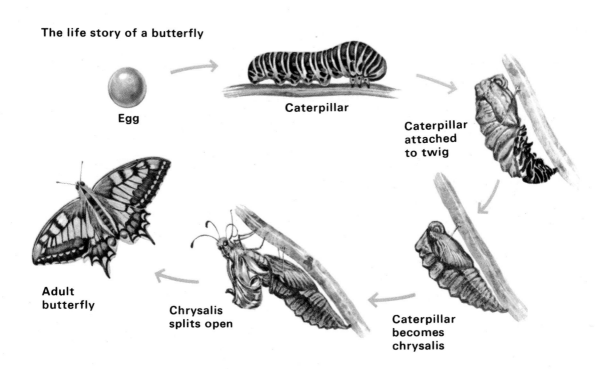

Egg

Caterpillar

Caterpillar
attached
to twig

Adult
butterfly

Chrysalis
splits open

Caterpillar
becomes
chrysalis

**Inside its silk
cocoon**

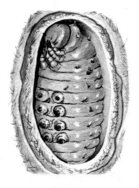

**the caterpillar is
becoming a moth.
You can see its
wings**

Butterflies and moths

Butterflies are the most beautiful insects. Like moths, butterflies have large wings. Their wings are often brightly coloured with beautiful patterns. The colours come from little scales all over the wings.

Life stories

Butterflies and moths start their lives as eggs. Each egg turns into a larva, called a caterpillar. The caterpillar feeds on leaves. It changes its skin several times as it grows and then turns into a pupa, called a chrysalis. The chrysalis rests for some time while its body slowly changes. Then, the chrysalis skin splits and the adult insect comes out. It waits for its body to get hard and for its wings to dry. Then it can fly away to visit the flowers for some food. Some caterpillars spin a cocoon of silk round themselves before they turn into chrysalides.

Feeding

Butterflies and moths feed on nectar. They suck the nectar from the flowers with a long tube, called a proboscis.

Butterfly or moth?

It is often hard to tell butterflies and moths apart. But it is quite easy if you remember that usually moths fly at night and butterflies fly during the day. Also, a butterfly usually has knobs on the ends of its feelers. Most moths do not.

The hummingbird hawk moth has a very long proboscis to suck the nectar from flowers

Some beautiful butterflies

Fiery acrea

Zebra swallowtail

Smokey orange tip

Rainbow

Ulysses

Camberwell beauty

Regent skipper

Adonis blue

Small copper

Brimstone

Silver-barred charaxes

Birdwing

Monarch

29

Social insects

Some insects live together and help each other. They are called 'social' insects. 'Social' means friendly and helpful.

The honeybee

Honeybees live in nests. In each nest there is one queen bee. She is the biggest. There are many worker bees who do all the work. The male bees, or drones, do no work at all.

The nest has thousands of wax cells, called honeycombs. The cells are like the rooms in a house. They are used for different purposes. Honey is stored in some of them and pollen in others.

The honeybee's nest is made of wax

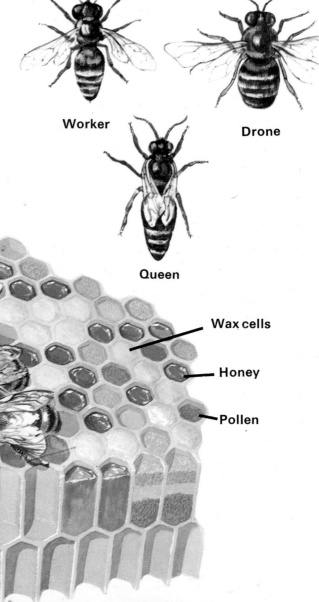

Worker

Drone

Queen

Workers

Queen

Wax cells

Honey

Pollen

Egg

Larva   Pupa   Young bee

Swarm of bees

The queen lays her eggs in the empty cells. She sometimes lays over a thousand eggs in one day. The eggs hatch into small white grubs. The young workers feed the queen and look after the grubs. The older workers go out and collect nectar and pollen from the flowers. They carry the pollen in baskets on their legs.

When the grubs have eaten enough food, the workers cover the cells with wax. Inside the cells the grubs turn into bees. They then bite their way through the wax covers. They are fed by the workers until they are strong.

Soon the queen's family becomes too big for the nest. So she leaves the nest, taking with her many of the worker bees and a few drones. They fly with her in a swarm. The other bees stay behind in the nest and wait for a new queen to hatch. The swarm flies on until the bees find a good place to build a new nest.

Outside of wasps' nest

Wasps

Some wasps are also social insects. The hornet's nest is made of paper. There are hundreds of cells inside and a door at the bottom. The hornet queen kills other insects and feeds them to her young grubs. When the grubs grow up they will go out and kill insects for themselves.

Inside of wasps' nest

Male

Queen
(with wings)

Worker

Ants

Ants are very clever animals. Most ants build wonderful nests. The wood ant makes an ant-hill from earth and dead leaves. Inside there are many rooms and tunnels. Thousands of ants live in the nest. Most of them are workers who scamper about looking after the eggs and the young ants. There are a few male ants but they do not do any work. The queen stays in the middle of the nest and lays all the eggs.

When the queen lays her eggs the workers take them to a special room where they will be safe and warm. They carry the eggs in their mouths. If the nest is disturbed the workers rush to hide the eggs and defend the young ants. Special big ants, called guards, make a circle round the nest. They fight the attackers.

The wood ants' nest is full of tunnels and rooms

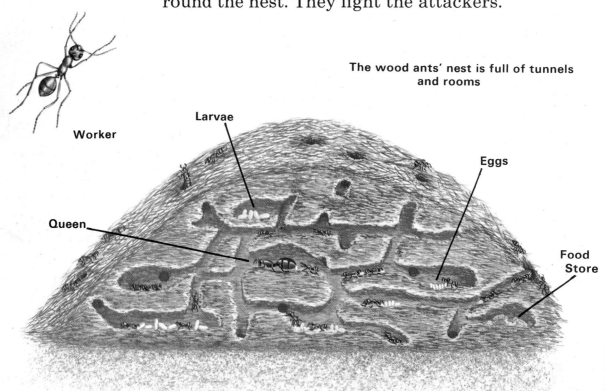

Larvae

Eggs

Queen

Food Store

Honey ants

These ants live in dry lands. Special workers hang from the top of the nest. Other ants feed them with honey and they store it in their bodies. When the ants run short of food the special workers have plenty for them.

Ant 'farmers'

Some ants feed on a kind of honey which they get by stroking greenflies. They milk the greenflies like cows.

The honeypot ant stores honey in its body

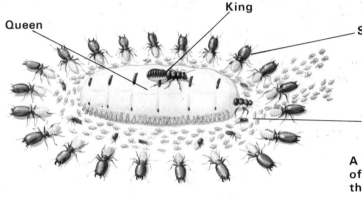

Queen · King · Soldiers · Workers

A termite nest is often much bigger than a man

Termites

Termites make huge mud nests. Some of their nests are bigger than a man. The king and queen live in the middle of the nest. The queen lays millions of eggs. The eggs turn into workers and soldiers. The workers make the nest bigger and feed the young termites. The soldiers guard the nest.

Insect pests

Most insects are quite harmless but some are pests. Some carry diseases which can kill men and animals. Others eat plants and spread plant diseases. A swarm of locusts will eat every green leaf for miles around. Crops of vegetables are eaten by caterpillars, and flowers are destroyed by greenflies.

The cockroach likes warm kitchens. It comes out at night and eats everything it can get in its jaws. The larvae of the clothes moth eat holes in clothes as they hang in the wardrobe. Fleas and lice live as parasites on the skin of animals. They spread many diseases.

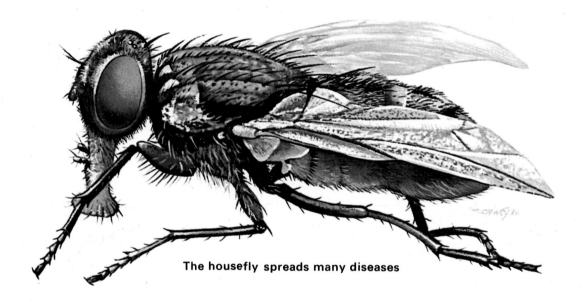

The housefly spreads many diseases

Flies

Flies are the most dangerous insects. They spread many diseases, including cholera and typhoid. Houseflies and blowflies feed on rotting food. As they buzz around rubbish dumps they may pick up germs and carry them back to our food. Tsetse-flies live in hot countries. They carry a disease called sleeping-sickness.

The mosquito carries malaria and yellow fever. The female mosquito feeds on the blood of other animals. She pierces the skin and sucks up blood through a long tube.

Boring beetle

Beetles

Many beetles do a lot of damage to wood. Some bore under the bark of trees. The woodworm beetle often lays its eggs in tiny cracks in furniture. The larvae may feed on the wood for three years before coming out as adults.

The larvae of the cockchafer and the click beetles tunnel in the soil and feed on the roots of crops.

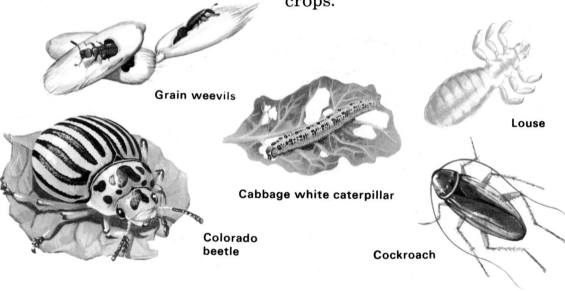

Grain weevils

Cabbage white caterpillar

Louse

Colorado beetle

Cockroach

The Colorado beetle attacks potatoes and other crops. It is so harmful that laws have been made to stamp it out. The Japanese beetle lives in America. It eats 250 different kinds of plants. Grain weevils and other small beetles destroy tons and tons of dried grain and flour every year.

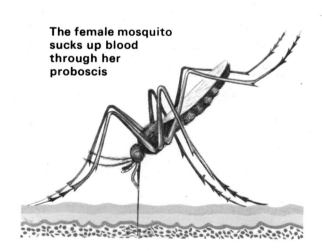

The female mosquito sucks up blood through her proboscis

Spiders

Abdomen

Palps

Legs

Spinnerets

Spiders are not insects. They have eight legs and their bodies are in two parts. Most spiders have more than two eyes but they still cannot see very well. They feel their way with their legs and with feelers, called palps. The spider has claws like small combs. It uses them to hold its prey.

The body and face of the garden spider

Palps

Eyes

Fangs

A garden spider's web

Webs

All spiders make silk. Some spiders use the silk to make webs. If you go out early on an autumn day, you may see a garden spider's web. The web is made from thousands of silk threads. It is a perfect trap for small insects. The funnel web spider makes a web on the ground. It is held by strong silk ropes. The spider sits at the bottom and waits for an insect to trip over the ropes. The house spider's web is just a tangled mass of silk.

Tarantulas live in
Southern Europe

Hunting spiders

Not all spiders make webs. Some live in holes in the ground
and come out to hunt at night. The tarantula is a wolf spider.
It runs down its prey and poisons it with its fangs. Tarantulas
look very fierce but their poison does not kill people.

Trapdoor spiders

Trapdoor spiders make sure that their homes are not invaded
by making a door to keep out their enemies. One spider makes a
door like a cork. The door is made of layers of silk and soil.
It is very hard to open the door because the spider holds on
to the inside.

A trapdoor spider. The door of its nest
is like a cork

Crab spiders

Crab spiders have a clever way of catching food. They hide in flowers and catch insects which come for the nectar. The insects do not see them because they are the same colour as the flowers.

Crab spiders get their name from the way they walk. Like crabs they can walk sideways and even backwards.

A hidden crab spider catches a beetle

Bird-eating spiders

Some of these hairy creatures are as big as a man's hand. They can kill small animals, such as mice and birds. There are tiny hairs on their backs which would make your hand very sore if you picked one up.

Bird-eating spider

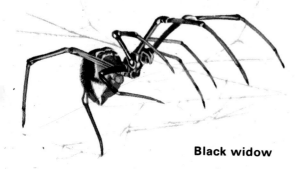
Black widow

Black widow

The black widow spider is a very dangerous spider which lives in America. It is small, shiny and black. Its bite can kill a man.

Scorpions

The scorpion is a relative of the spider. It lives mostly in dry lands. It has a long tail which bends over its body. At the end of its tail there is a poisonous sting. Some scorpions can even kill a man with their poison. Scorpions can run very fast and they have big claws.

Scorpion

Mites and ticks

These little creatures are cousins of the spiders. Ticks are pests. They feed on animals and spread diseases. Many mites also feed on animals and damage plants.

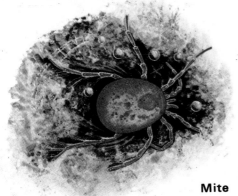
Mite

Harvestmen

Harvestmen are also related to spiders. They have very long legs. Many harvestmen live near water. They die if there is no water to drink. They eat insects but they cannot poison them as spiders do.

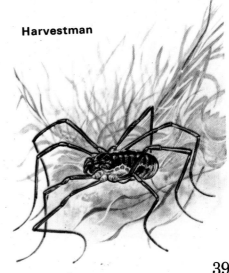
Harvestman

Green seaweed

Life on the Seashore

When the tide is out the seashore is crowded with plants and animals. On sandy or muddy beaches the animals bury themselves to keep out of the sun. Rocky beaches are more interesting. The animals shelter in rock pools and are easy to see.

Rock pools

In a rock pool you can look at plants and animals which usually live in the sea. Winkles hide in cracks in the rocks and fishes shelter among the seaweed. Shrimps, crabs, starfishes, barnacles and sea-anemones are often left behind when the tide goes out.

Brown seaweed

Red seaweed

Seaweed

Seaweeds are plants that grow in the sea near the shore. They do not have flowers. There are three kinds of seaweed – green, brown and red. Sea lettuce is a common green seaweed. It grows on rocks which are uncovered when the tide goes out. Tangleweed is a brown seaweed which grows in deeper water. Most seaweeds soon dry up and die if they are out of the water for too long. Bladder wrack is often called 'pop weed' because it has bumps on its leaves which pop when they are squeezed.

Periwinkles sheltering in the bladder wrack

Barnacles

The rocks on the seashore are often covered with little cone-shaped barnacles. A barnacle can open and close its shell.

Sea-anemones

Sea-anemones are strange animals. They have a mouth surrounded by tentacles which open like flowers when the tide is in. When the tide is out they close up. They look like blobs of jelly.

When the tide is in the sea-anemones and the barnacles put out their tentacles to catch food

Barnacle

Sea-anemone

Blenny

Fishes

Look in a rock pool and you may see fishes that have been left behind by the tide. The blenny has a long fin along its back. It feeds on barnacles and worms. Hiding among the seaweed or under rocks you may also find gobies and sea-scorpions.

Worms

Worms bury themselves in the sand when the tide is out. Ragworms are covered in bristles. They can swim in the sea. The peacock worm lives in a tube buried in the sand. When the water covers the beach it spreads out its tentacles to catch food. Some worms live in tiny tubes on stones.

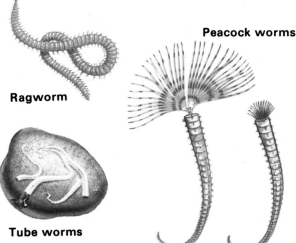
Ragworm

Tube worms

Peacock worms

Crabs

Most crabs live in the sea near the shore. Some crabs shelter in rock pools or under seaweed. Nearly all crabs have hard shells. They move with a funny side-ways walk. Crabs are scavengers. They pick up scraps of food with their long claws. The spider crab has very long, thin legs. The little edible crab lives on the beach in summer. In winter it goes back to the sea.

Spider crab

Edible crab

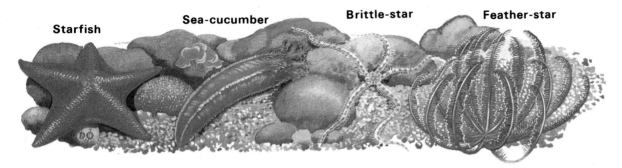

Starfish   **Sea-cucumber**   **Brittle-star**   **Feather-star**

Starfishes and their relatives

You can easily tell a starfish by its five broad arms.
The starfish has many relatives, including
brittle-stars, sea-urchins, sea-cucumbers and
sea-lilies. They usually live on the sea bed
but sometimes they are washed up on the beach.
The starfish and its relatives all have spiny
skins. Many of them have hundreds of little
'tube-feet' with suckers on them. They use the
suckers to pull themselves along. Sea-urchins
look like hard, spiky balls. They move along on
their long spines.

Sea-lily

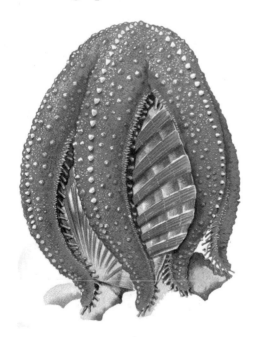

Starfishes can pull open mollusc shells
with their strong arms and tube feet

The sea-lily looks like a
plant. It has a long 'stalk'
and pretty tentacles round its
mouth.

Starfishes often feed on
cockles and mussels. They
grip the shells with their tube-
feet and pull them apart. If a
starfish's arm breaks off, it can
grow a new one.

Many members of the
starfish family bury themselves
in the sand to hide from their
enemies.

Jellyfishes

Jellyfishes float near the surface of the sea. They look like blobs of jelly. Many of them are brightly coloured. The body of the common jellyfish is shaped like an umbrella with a fringe of tentacles hanging round its mouth.
It catches its food with its tentacles. At the end of the tentacles are painful stings which the jellyfish uses to stun the animals on which it feeds. The Portuguese man-o'-war is huge. It is really lots of jellyfishes joined together. Its sting is very dangerous.

Birds

Many birds live on the coast and feed on fishes. Most of them nest on cliffs and beaches. They have webbed feet to swim with. Gannets and cormorants dive into the sea after fish. They can swim underwater. Gulls feed on tit-bits lying on the beach. In bad weather they often fly far inland in search of food. Puffins nest in burrows in the cliffs. They often use a rabbit's burrow or dig a new one with their beaks. They scoop away the earth with their feet.

Portuguese
man-o'-war

Common
jellyfish

Puffin

Oystercatcher

Gannet

Cormorant

Sea shells

You can find many kinds of shells washed up on a beach. Most of them are empty because the snails which once lived in them have died. Shells are movable homes or hide-aways for animals called molluscs. Their bodies are very soft and weak. The hard shells protect them from their enemies and stop the sun drying up their bodies. Each mollusc has its own shape of shell. Some are very pretty. Some are very big. The giant clam weighs as much as four men. Some beaches are made of millions of shells instead of sand or pebbles.

Oysters

Oysters are the best-known molluscs. The oyster makes a beautiful lining inside its shell. The lining is called mother-of-pearl. If a grain of sand gets inside the shell, it hurts the oyster. So the oyster covers the rough sand with mother-of-pearl to make it smooth. It makes a pearl.

Oysters are very good to eat. But oysters with pearls in them are valued even more.

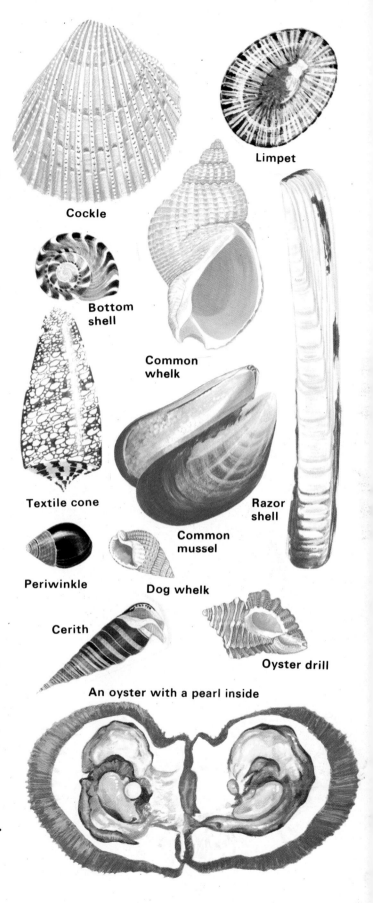

Cockle

Limpet

Bottom shell

Common whelk

Textile cone

Razor shell

Common mussel

Periwinkle

Dog whelk

Cerith

Oyster drill

An oyster with a pearl inside

Life in the Sea

Many people think that all the animals in the sea are fish. This is not true. Whales are not fish. Nor are the tiny planktonic animals.

Plankton

Planktonic animals and plants are so small that you can see them only through a microscope. But they have beautiful colours and patterns. They live mostly at the top of the sea, where the tiny plants use the sunlight to make food. The animals cannot make food so they eat the tiny plants.

Herring

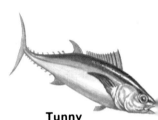

Tunny

Plankton magnified thousands of times

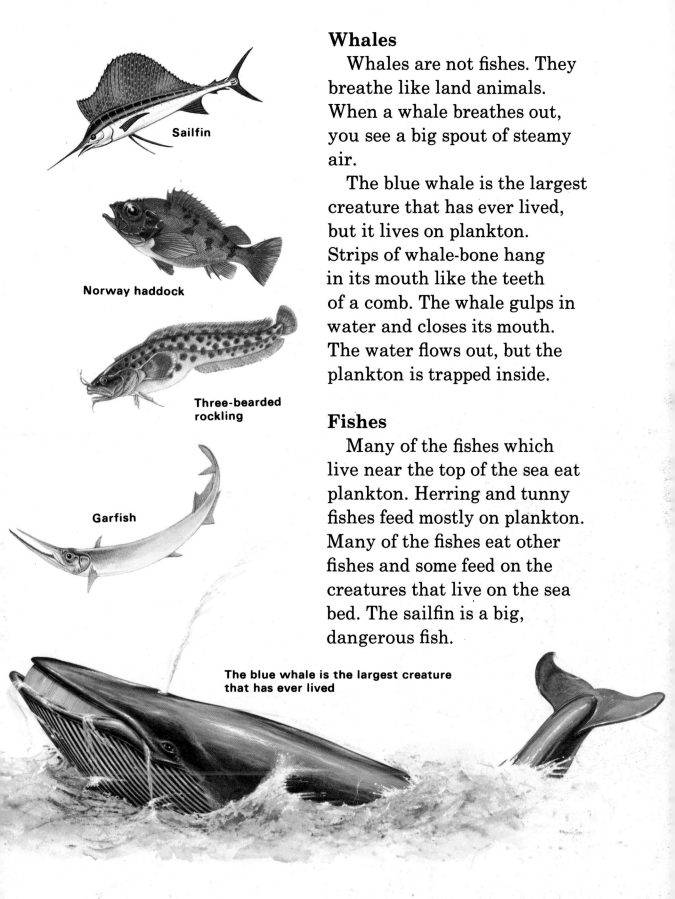

Sailfin

Norway haddock

Three-bearded
rockling

Garfish

Whales

Whales are not fishes. They breathe like land animals. When a whale breathes out, you see a big spout of steamy air.

The blue whale is the largest creature that has ever lived, but it lives on plankton. Strips of whale-bone hang in its mouth like the teeth of a comb. The whale gulps in water and closes its mouth. The water flows out, but the plankton is trapped inside.

Fishes

Many of the fishes which live near the top of the sea eat plankton. Herring and tunny fishes feed mostly on plankton. Many of the fishes eat other fishes and some feed on the creatures that live on the sea bed. The sailfin is a big, dangerous fish.

The blue whale is the largest creature
that has ever lived

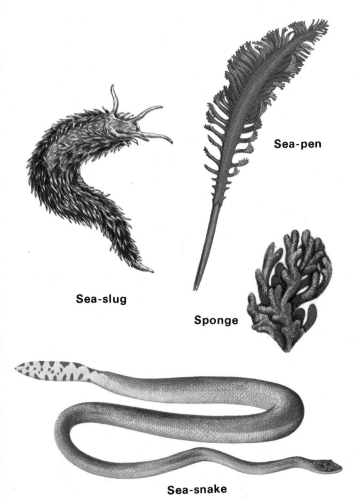

Sea-slug

Sea-pen

Sponge

Sea-snake

The sea bed

All kinds of strange animals live on the bottom of the sea. Sea-slugs and starfishes hide in the great forests of seaweed near the shore. Lobsters and crabs crawl along the bottom, passing the flatfishes lying almost invisible on the sea bed. Rays 'fly' through the water, flapping their wing-like fins.

The sting-ray defends itself with the poisonous spikes in its tail. Pretty sea snakes live on the bottom of some tropical seas. They have flat tails like the blade of an oar. They are very poisonous. Sponges look like plants growing on the sea bed. But they are really animals.

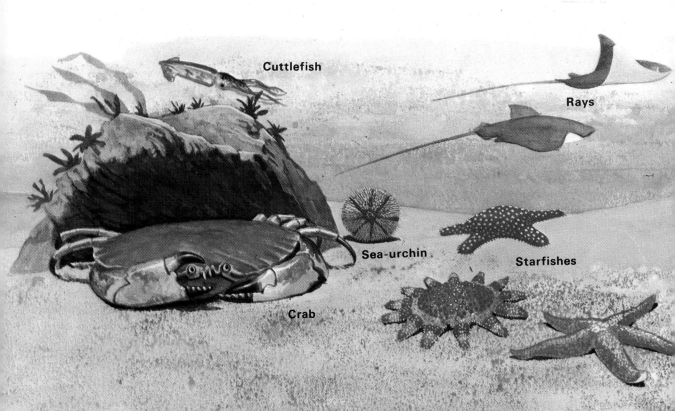

Cuttlefish

Rays

Sea-urchin

Starfishes

Crab

Octopuses and their relatives

Octopuses, squids and cuttlefish belong to the same family. They catch other animals with the long tentacles which grow from their heads. The tentacles have suckers on them. It is very easy to hurt an octopus or a squid because their skin is so soft. But it is sometimes very hard to see them because they can change the colour of their skin to match their background. When an octopus or a squid is disturbed it squirts a dark, inky liquid into the water. This hides the animal while it escapes from its enemy. Most members of the octopus family can move backwards by shooting out a jet of water from a funnel among their tentacles. Some squids grow to an enormous size. They even fight fierce battles with the great sperm whales.

Octopus

Deep-sea fishes

Far down in the deepest part of the sea live all sorts of strange fishes. They are called deep-sea fishes. No plants can grow in these dark waters so the fishes eat one another. Because it is so dark many deep-sea fishes make their own light. This light helps them to hunt for food. The ugly angler fish has a shining 'fishing rod' on its head. The light attracts fishes into its huge mouth.

Corals

Corals are small, jelly-like animals that live in warm seas. They have tiny tentacles to catch food. Corals build little stone 'cups', or skeletons, round themselves to protect their soft bodies. The skeleton is left behind when the animal dies. Slowly millions of the skeletons build up into a great wall called a coral reef.

Seahorses

The seahorse has a head that looks like a horse's head. It hooks itself to corals and seaweeds with its long tail.

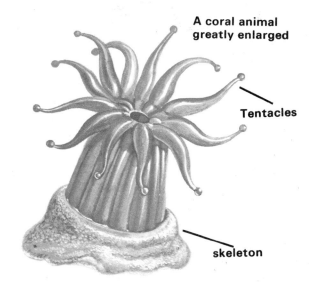

A coral animal greatly enlarged

Tentacles

skeleton

The tiny coral animal has tentacles round its mouth and a hard skeleton which protects its body. Corals often live in colonies. They look like pretty plants

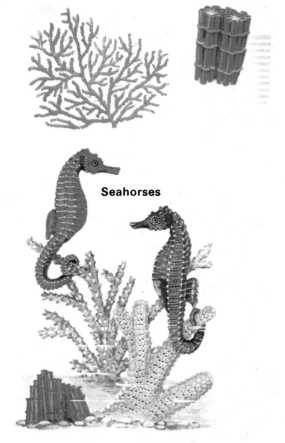

Seahorses

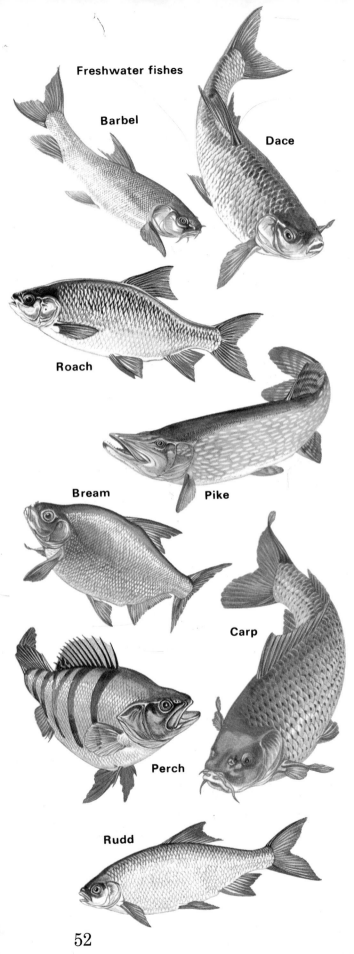

Freshwater fishes

Barbel

Dace

Roach

Bream

Pike

Carp

Perch

Rudd

Fishes

Fishes spend all their lives in water. They breathe by taking oxygen from the water with their gills. Their bodies are shaped so that they can move easily through the water. Most fishes also have fins. The tail fin drives the fish through the water. The other fins help it to turn and to keep its balance.

Inside the fish's body there is often a swim-bladder. This is a kind of bag which has gas in it. By changing the amount of gas the fish can sink or rise in the water.

There are fishes all over the world but not all fishes can live in the same kind of water.

Freshwater fishes

Freshwater fishes live in rivers, streams, lakes or ponds. The largest family of freshwater fishes is the carp family. In summer the water in rivers and ponds gets warm quickly. In winter the water may get very cold and freeze. Then the carp buries itself in the mud at the bottom of the water and goes to sleep.

Saltwater fishes

Some fishes can only live in the sea where the water is salty. Many of them are caught for food. Cod, herring and mackerel are important food fishes. Herrings swim near the top of the sea. They eat plankton. The mackerel lives in deeper water. It swims very fast to catch other fishes for its food. The cod feeds mostly on other fishes. It also eats worms and molluscs living on the sea bed. Each year the cod lays millions of eggs but most of them are eaten by other fishes. Perhaps only six out of six million will survive.

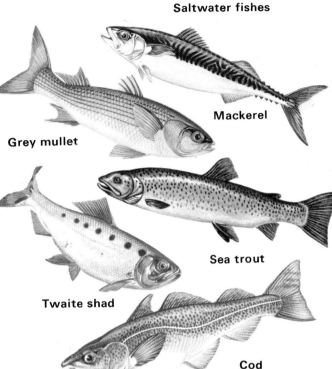

Saltwater fishes

Mackerel

Grey mullet

Sea trout

Twaite shad

Cod

Greater weaver

Stages in the life of the salmon

Eggs

Larva (fry)

Young salmon (parr)

Adult salmon

The salmon

Salmon start their lives in quiet streams. After about two years the young salmon swims down the river to the sea. It lives in the sea for several years. Then it returns to the river to lay its eggs. It has to leap rapids and waterfalls because the water is flowing against it. By the time it reaches the end of its long journey, the salmon is worn out. It is thin and has lost its colour. Once it has laid its eggs it usually dies.

Stages in the life of the plaice

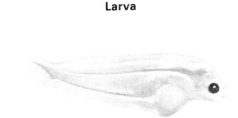

Larva

Head grows to one side

Both eyes on top

Adult plaice

Flatfishes

Flatfishes live on the sea bed. There are about 600 kinds of flatfishes. The halibut is the largest. Some halibuts are bigger than a man. Other flatfishes are the plaice, flounder, dab, sole and turbot. These fishes all grow in the same way.

When it is very young the fish is the same shape as other fish. But after a while its head grows more on one side than the other, so that both eyes are on the same side of its body.

The top side of a flatfish's body is coloured. But the colour does not stay the same. Flatfishes can change their colour to match their background. If you put a plaice on a chess board, it will go black and white.

Eels

Eels are long, thin fishes. The common eel lays its eggs in the sea but spends most of its life in rivers. Conger eels live in the sea near the coast of Europe. They are the largest eels. Moray eels are very fierce. They live in warm, shallow seas.

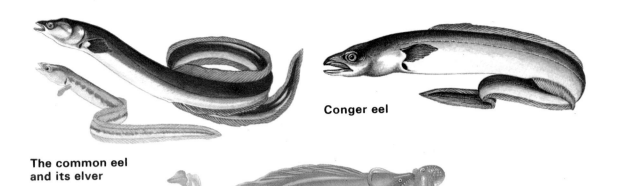

The common eel and its elver

Conger eel

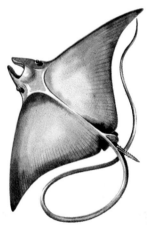

Moray eel eating an octopus

Sharks and rays

Sharks are the most frightening fishes. They have large mouths with rows of sharp teeth. Their bodies are long and have a large fin on the back. This fin often sticks out of the water, giving the first sign that there are sharks nearby.

The largest shark is the whale shark, but it is quite harmless to man. Man-eating sharks include the white shark, leopard shark, tiger shark and blue shark.

Rays are related to sharks. They have wide, flat bodies. Manta rays are often 20 feet wide. They are called devil fish, although they are quite harmless. The sting ray has a poisonous spine on its tail.

The manta ray is also called the devil fish. It may be twenty feet wide and it can leap out of the water

Blue shark

Thresher shark

55

Electric fishes

Long before people learned how to make electricity, there were fishes which could produce electric shocks. The torpedo ray is the most famous electric fish. One part of its body is like the battery of a torch, but it does not use it to make light. It uses it to attack its enemies and to catch food. The electric eel can give the most powerful shock. It is so strong that it can stun a man.

Deep-sea fishes

These fishes belong to many different families, but they are all alike in some ways. They all have thin bones and very thin skins. You can see right through their bodies. Most of them can make their own light.

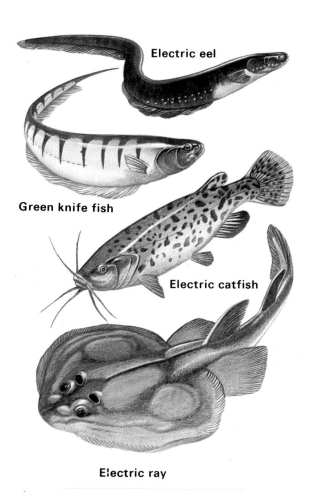

Electric eel

Green knife fish

Electric catfish

Electric ray

Deep-sea fishes look very fierce but most of them are no bigger than your thumb

56

Tropical fishes

Tropical fishes live in warm seas and rivers. Many of them have beautiful patterns and colours on their bodies. Their enemies can see them easily, but they protect themselves by hiding among the corals which are also brightly coloured. Many of them can also change their colours very quickly.

Some tropical fishes do not lay eggs. The guppy gives birth to live young. But sometimes it eats all its young. Many people keep guppies and other tropical fishes in an aquarium.

Keeping an aquarium

An aquarium is a tank for keeping fishes and other water animals. Goldfish are easy to keep in an aquarium. If you want to keep tropical fish, the water in the tank must be kept warm. The bottom of the tank should be covered with sand. The water must be kept clean. Fishes also need oxygen to breathe. If you keep water plants in the tank, they will supply oxygen for the fishes.

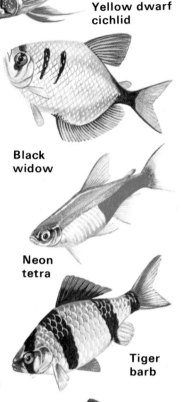

Yellow dwarf cichlid

Black widow

Neon tetra

Tiger barb

Midnight molly

Tropical fishes live happily in an aquarium if the water is kept warm and clean

Life in Ponds and Streams

Ponds are the homes of many plants and animals. Rushes, reeds and flowers grow by the water's edge. In deeper water there are water lilies, frogbit, pondweed and duckweed. The small plants float on the water. The larger ones are rooted to the bottom by long stems. The plants provide food and oxygen for the fishes and other animals.

Some of the animals do not have to get air from the water. Many bugs, beetles and snails carry their own air with them. The water boatman swims through the water on its back. It uses its long legs like paddles. In the mud at the bottom of the pond there are many snails, worms and mussels.

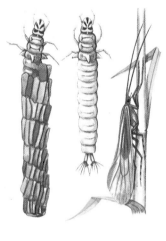

Caddis fly and larva

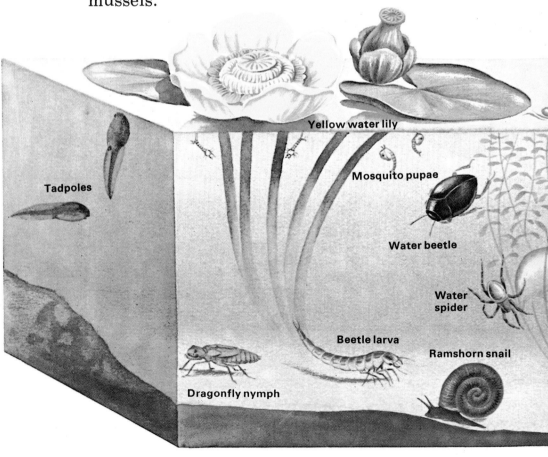

Yellow water lily

Mosquito pupae

Water beetle

Water spider

Tadpoles

Beetle larva

Ramshorn snail

Dragonfly nymph

58

The dragonfly lays its eggs in a pond or stream. The nymphs have no wings and live in the water. They breathe through gills and feed on other water creatures. After a year or more the nymph climbs up a reed and sheds its skin. It flies away as an adult dragonfly.

The caddis fly also lays its eggs in water. As soon as the larva hatches, it builds itself a case to live in. It uses bits of plants or tiny shells and sand to make the case.

Dragonflies have good eyesight. They catch insects in flight

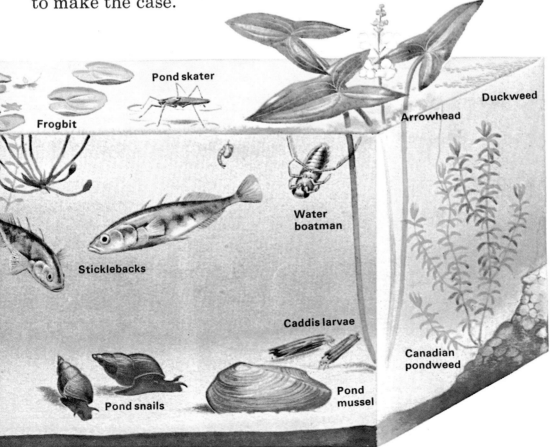

Frogbit

Pond skater

Arrowhead

Duckweed

Sticklebacks

Water boatman

Caddis larvae

Canadian pondweed

Pond snails

Pond mussel

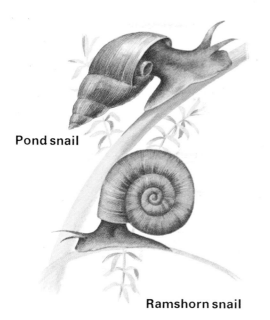

Pond snail

Ramshorn snail

Pond skater

The pond skater is a bug with long, thin legs. It lives on the top of the pond. The surface of the water acts like a thin skin which can bear its weight. As it skates across the water, it feeds on insects which have fallen into the pond.

Geometric leech

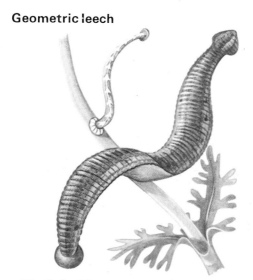

Medicinal leech

Snails and mussels

Some water snails have lungs. They have to go to the surface to get air. Some have gills. They can get air from the water like fishes. Water snails scrape up tiny plants from the stones with their rough tongues.

Freshwater mussels help to keep the water in the pond clear. They eat bacteria and the slimy microscopic plants.

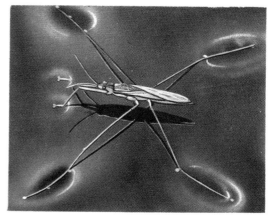

Pond skater

Worms and leeches

Many different kinds of worms live in ponds. Some burrow in the mud and make mud tubes in which to live. Leeches are worms. They attach themselves to stones or weeds. They have suckers at each end of their bodies. Leeches live on the blood of other animals. They suck blood from frogs, fishes and snails.

Fishes

Many fishes which live in ponds and streams taste nasty, because there is so much mud in the water. The pike is a large, ugly fish. It feeds on fishes, voles, birds and anything else it can swallow.

Bleak

Gudgeon

Birds

Many birds make their homes by the banks of streams and ponds. The reeds make safe hide-outs for their nests. There are lots of fishes, worms, insects, snails and waterweeds for them to eat. Ducks, grebes, moorhens and coots nest among the reeds and there are swans, herons and dippers.

Moorhen

Mammals

A few mammals live by the water's edge. There are beavers, otters, musk rats, coypus, water shrews and water voles. Most of these animals are good swimmers. The water shrew has a long, pointed nose. It swims under the water looking for insects to eat.

Water shrews

Dabchick

Mallard

Coot

Amphibians

Amphibians are animals which can live on the land or in the water. Frogs and toads are amphibians. So are salamanders, newts and apodans.

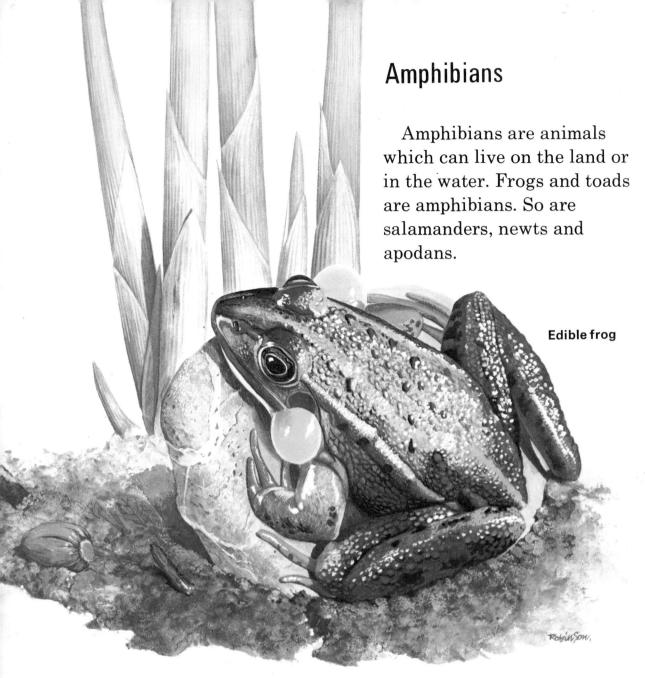

Edible frog

Frogs

Frogs begin life underwater. In spring, the female frog lays hundreds of eggs. They are covered in jelly. A clump of eggs is called frog-spawn. In a few days the eggs hatch into tiny tadpoles. At first the tadpole has no eyes and mouth. Soon it grows a mouth and begins to eat tiny plants. It has a tail for swimming and gills for breathing.

Frog-spawn

Tadpole hatches

Gills grow

Tadpole breathes through inner gills

Back legs grow

Front legs grow

Froglet

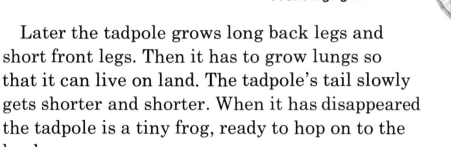

Later the tadpole grows long back legs and short front legs. Then it has to grow lungs so that it can live on land. The tadpole's tail slowly gets shorter and shorter. When it has disappeared the tadpole is a tiny frog, ready to hop on to the land.

The development of a frog

The fully grown frog has a smooth, slimy skin. It has a long, sticky tongue. When it sees a tasty fly, the frog shoots out its tongue and, in a second, the insect is swallowed whole.

Most frogs like to live in damp places. Some frogs live in trees. They have long 'fingers' with sticky pads on them for climbing.

Most frogs are harmless but the arrow poison frog is very dangerous. The Indians of South America used to put its poison on the tips of their arrows when they went out hunting.

Arrow poison frog

European tree frog

Natterjack toad

Toads

Toads are rather like frogs, but their skin is rough and bumpy. It is covered in warts.

Toads lay their eggs in strings. The eggs turn into tadpoles. When the tiny toads leave the water they stay by the pond, hiding under leaves and stones.

The natterjack toad digs a hole in the ground and stays in it during the day. It comes out at night to catch food. It does not hop like other frogs and toads. It walks on all four legs.

Most toads have poison glands. If an animal catches a toad in its mouth, the poison flows out on to the toad's skin. One taste of the poison and the animal will drop the toad.

Fire salamander

64

Newts

Newts spend much of their time in the water. Like frogs they can breathe through their skins. They have long tails to swim with and four short legs for moving about on land. When the female has laid her eggs, the adult newts usually leave the water. They spend the summer on land. In winter, newts and other amphibians stay underground to keep warm

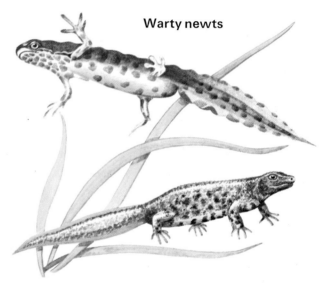

Warty newts

Salamanders

Most salamanders are small, shy animals. They live under stones during the day and hunt for worms and insects at night. Salamanders often have beautiful patterns on their skins.

Some salamanders never grow up. Axolotls, olms and mud puppies are salamanders but they remain tadpoles all their lives.

Apodans

The apodan looks like a large earthworm. It has no legs and it lives in the earth. It only comes out when it is raining. If it stayed underground it would drown. Apodans are often called 'blindworms' because they have no eyes.

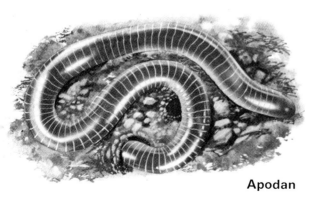

Apodan

Tortoise

Reptiles

Millions of years ago the world was ruled by the largest land animals that have ever lived. They were the great dinosaurs. The dinosaurs were reptiles. There are no dinosaurs now, but there are still many reptiles.

Turtles, lizards, snakes and crocodiles are all reptiles.

Turtles and tortoises

Turtles and tortoises have shells like great suits of armour. When they are in danger they can pull in their legs and heads.

Tortoises live on land but they can only move slowly because their shells are so heavy. In the Galapagos Islands there are some giant tortoises. Many of them are over a hundred years old.

Green turtle

Sea turtles spend their lives in the water, but they lay their eggs on land. Often they return to the same place where they were born. The female turtle leaves the water and drags herself up the beach. She digs a hole with her flippers and lays her eggs in it. Then she covers the eggs with sand and makes her way back to the sea. She leaves the eggs to hatch in the warm sun. After a time the little turtles dig their way out of the sand and crawl down the beach to the sea.

Some turtles live in ponds and streams. They are often called terrapins.

Marine iguana

Lizards

There are about 2,500 different kinds of
lizards. Their skin is covered in scales and
most of them have long tails. When an animal
catches a lizard by its tail, the tail usually
drops off and the lizard escapes. But it is
not long before a new tail grows. Lizards are
cold-blooded animals. They have to bury
themselves in cold weather to keep warm.

Most lizards are small but
there are some very large ones.
The komodo dragon is bigger
than a man. Another large
lizard is the marine iguana.
It lives on the shores of the
Galapagos Islands. It eats
seaweed.

Tegu lizard

The gila monster lives in America.
Unlike most lizards, it is poisonous. The
Australian frilled lizard is harmless but it
has a good way of scaring its enemies. It has
a fold of loose skin round its shoulders.
When it is afraid it makes the 'frill' stiff.
It looks so fierce that its attacker is
frightened away.

Australian frilled lizard

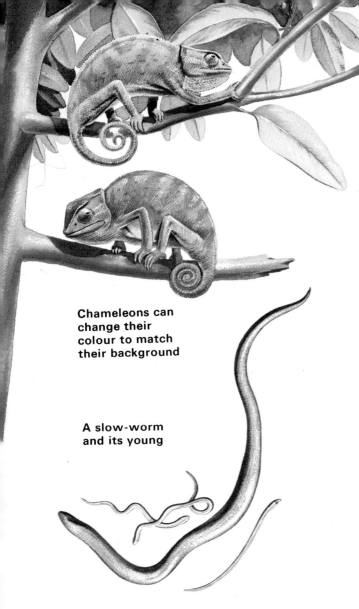

Chameleons

Chameleons live in trees. They have long, sticky tongues which they shoot out to catch insects. Like many other lizards, the chameleon protects itself from its enemies by changing the colour of its skin to match its background. It is very hard to find a chameleon when it is as green as the leaves it is hiding in.

Chameleons can change their colour to match their background

A slow-worm and its young

Slow-worms

Slow-worms look like snakes because they have no legs, but they are really lizards. They burrow in the earth eating insects and worms. The glass snake is also a legless lizard.

Tuatara

Tuatara

The tuatara is a strange reptile which lives in New Zealand. It is a very lazy animal. It does not move very fast and one breath may last it for more than half an hour. It hides during the day in a burrow. At night it hunts for insects and other small animals.

Grass snake

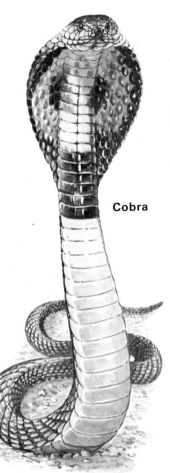
Cobra

Snakes

Even though they have no legs, snakes find it quite easy to move about and catch their food. Their long bodies are covered in scales. The snake presses the scales against the ground and pushes itself along.

The way snakes eat is very strange. They swallow their food whole even if it is larger than their own body. They can do this because their jaws are not tightly joined. They can stretch apart like elastic. One good meal lasts a snake a long time so they do not eat very often. The egg-eating snake can swallow great big eggs. When it has swallowed the egg it crushes it and spits out the shell.

The grass snake family

The grass snake belongs to the largest snake family. All its members are quite harmless.

The cobra family

Cobras and mambas have large fangs at the front of their mouths. They use their poison to defend themselves and to kill their prey. Most cobras have 'hoods'. When they are angry or afraid, they raise their hoods. Some of them spit poison at the attacker.

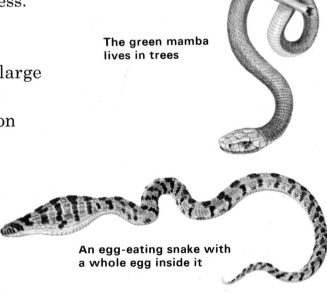
The green mamba lives in trees

An egg-eating snake with a whole egg inside it

69

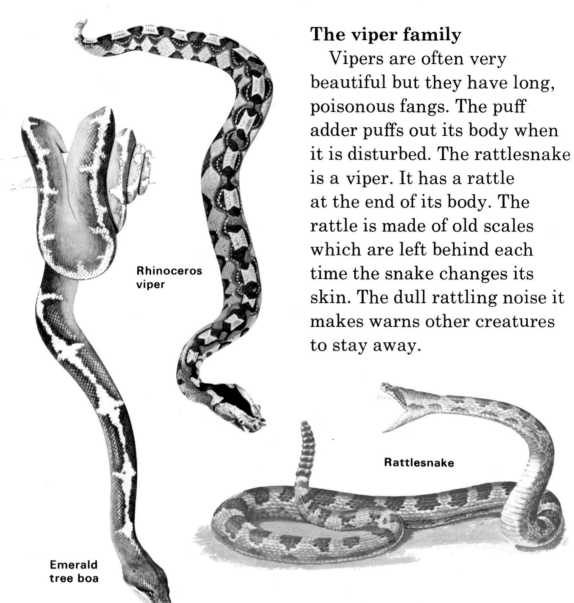

Rhinoceros viper

Emerald tree boa

Rattlesnake

The viper family

Vipers are often very beautiful but they have long, poisonous fangs. The puff adder puffs out its body when it is disturbed. The rattlesnake is a viper. It has a rattle at the end of its body. The rattle is made of old scales which are left behind each time the snake changes its skin. The dull rattling noise it makes warns other creatures to stay away.

Puff Adder

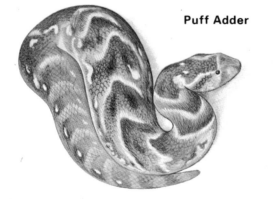

The boas and pythons

Boas and pythons are large snakes but they are not poisonous. They kill their prey by strangling it. The snake winds itself round the animal's body so that it cannot breathe. The giant anaconda is the largest member of the boa family. It is often over 30 feet long.

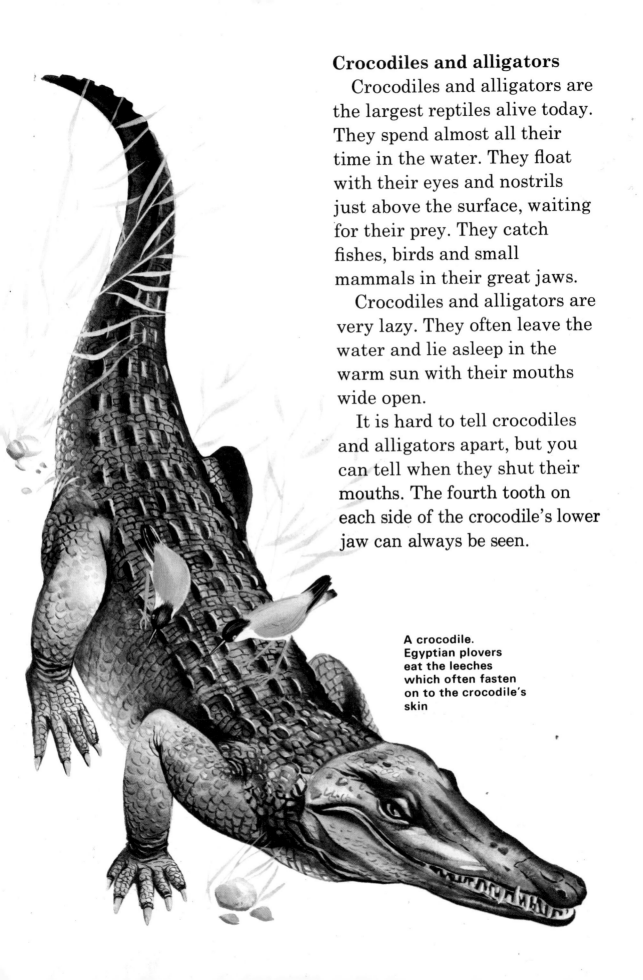

Crocodiles and alligators

Crocodiles and alligators are the largest reptiles alive today. They spend almost all their time in the water. They float with their eyes and nostrils just above the surface, waiting for their prey. They catch fishes, birds and small mammals in their great jaws.

Crocodiles and alligators are very lazy. They often leave the water and lie asleep in the warm sun with their mouths wide open.

It is hard to tell crocodiles and alligators apart, but you can tell when they shut their mouths. The fourth tooth on each side of the crocodile's lower jaw can always be seen.

A crocodile. Egyptian plovers eat the leeches which often fasten on to the crocodile's skin

Birds

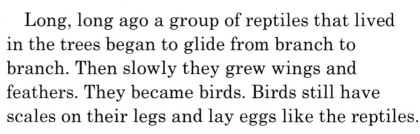

Long, long ago a group of reptiles that lived in the trees began to glide from branch to branch. Then slowly they grew wings and feathers. They became birds. Birds still have scales on their legs and lay eggs like the reptiles.

Baby shrikes

Australian lyre bird

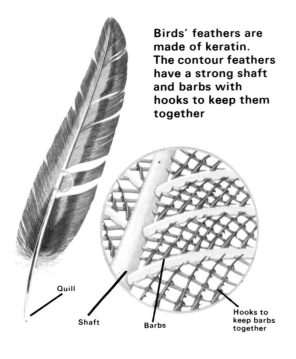

Birds' feathers are made of keratin. The contour feathers have a strong shaft and barbs with hooks to keep them together

Quill

Shaft

Barbs

Hooks to keep barbs together

Wings and feathers

All birds have wings. A wing is like a special arm. It is very light and it is shaped for flying. The bird has strong muscles to move its wings.

Birds have two kinds of feathers. Small, fluffy 'down' feathers cover the bird's body. They trap a layer of air next to the bird's skin to keep it warm. Contour feathers are larger. They cover the bird's body as well as its wings and tail.

72

Beaks

Birds do not have teeth. They have beaks. You can often tell what a bird eats from its beak. Hunting birds, like falcons, have sharp, hooked beaks for tearing flesh. The kingfisher has a beak like a dagger. It uses it to snatch fishes from the water. Some birds feed on worms and molluscs. They have long, curved beaks to dig in the mud. The humming birds have long, thin beaks to reach inside flowers for nectar. Many birds eat seeds and nuts. They have short, thick beaks so that they can crack hard shells. Some ducks have long, flat beaks. They scoop up mud in them and sift food into their mouths.

Feet

A bird's feet also tell us a lot about the kind of life it leads. The kingfisher has toes which can grip branches and dig. The heron spends most of its time wading on soft mud. It has long toes which are spread out so that it does not sink in the mud. Many water birds have flaps of skin between their toes. These 'webbed' feet are used for swimming.

Kingfisher

Heron

Duck

Humming bird

Bullfinch

Shoveller duck

Falcon

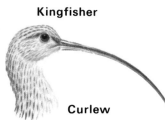

Kingfisher

Curlew

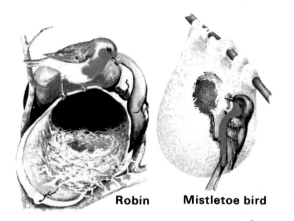

Robin   Mistletoe bird

Oven bird

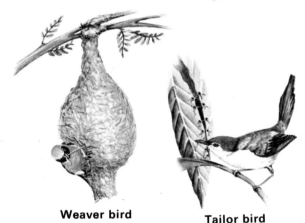

Weaver bird   Tailor bird

Nests

Most birds build nests to lay their eggs in. Different birds make different kinds of nests. The robin builds a nest of leaves and twigs and anything else it can find. It will make its nest almost anywhere that is safe and warm.

Some birds are very clever nest builders. The little tailor bird sews two leaves together with the stem of a plant to make a hanging nest. The weaver bird uses dry grass to make a nest shaped like a lantern. The oven bird makes its nest from mud. When the mud has dried in the sun, it is as hard as a brick house. The mistletoe bird builds a snow white nest at the top of a tree. It is made from cobwebs and the feathery 'down' from seeds.

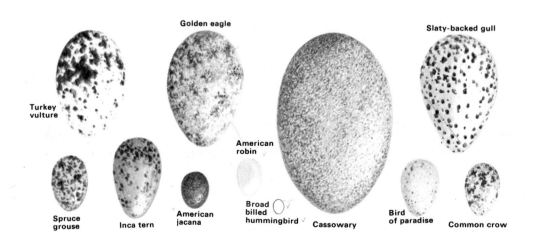

Turkey vulture

Golden eagle

American robin

Slaty-backed gull

Spruce grouse

Inca tern

American jacana

Broad billed hummingbird

Cassowary

Bird of paradise

Common crow

Cuckoo

The cuckoo does not bother to make a nest. It lays its eggs in the nests of other birds. The cuckoo always chooses a nest where the eggs look like her own. She takes one egg from the nest and lays her own in its place. Then she flies off with the stolen egg. When the mother bird returns she has no idea that there is a cuckoo egg in her nest. But as soon as the eggs hatch the cuckoo makes itself known. It forces all the other young birds out of the nest. There will not be enough food for them all. The mother bird then feeds and cares for the young cuckoo. It grows to be bigger than she is.

The cuckoo has laid her
egg in a whitethroat's nest

The whitethroat feeds the
young cuckoo

Migration

Sometimes one country is too cold for a bird to stay in all the year round. So it flies to another country. This movement is called migration. Each year the Arctic tern flies thousands of miles from one end of the world to the other. The swift flies from Britain to Africa. Many of the birds return to exactly the same place in which they nested the year before. Nobody is really sure how the birds find their way. But most experts believe that they use the sun and stars to guide them.

Albatross

Brown pelican

Cormorant

Skua

Shag

Diver

Sea Birds

The sea is the home of many birds. Most of them eat fish. The brown pelican plunges into the water with a great splash and scoops up fishes in its pouched beak. Gannets dive deep into the water from great heights. Skuas chase other birds and force them to drop the fish they have caught. Gulls are not very good at fishing, so they will eat almost anything.

The wandering albatross has longer wings than any other bird. It often soars over the ocean all day without a rest.

Ducks, geese and swans

Ducks, geese and swans all belong to the same family. They all have very beautiful feathers. Their 'down' feathers are very soft. They often line their nests with them. The eider duck uses so much 'down' for its nest that people collect the feathers. They use them to make bed covers, called eiderdowns.

When a male goose (gander) or swan has chosen his mate he stays with her for life.

Eider duck

Canada goose

Teal

Swan

Wading birds

Most wading birds have very long legs and long beaks. They live mostly on marshes and beaches. They dig in the mud for worms and insects. Some of them eat fishes, frogs and small mammals as well. The spoonbill has a broad, flat beak, called a bill. It wades through the water with its bill just under the surface ready to catch any tiny plants and animals. The flamingo has a curved bill. When it dips its bill into the water the top is underneath. It scoops up mud and eats any food in it. Then the rest is strained out through holes in the top of the bill.

Most of the wading birds have loud voices. The adult stork has no voice but it makes a loud noise by rattling its beak. Cranes are very happy birds. They like dancing. They often get together and bow and leap into the air.

Lined tiger heron

Agami heron

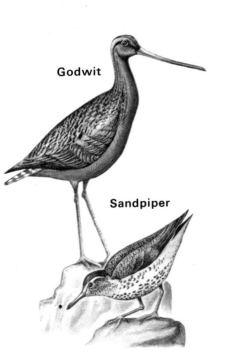

Godwit

Sandpiper

Crowned crane

Sarus crane

Roseate spoonbill

Scarlet ibis

Shrike

Black-naped oriole

Bee-eater

Bohemian waxwing

Great tit

Varied tit

Blue tit

Chough

Tree swallow

House sparrow

Winter wren

Perching birds

One group of birds has over 5,000 members. They are the perching birds, or songbirds. Most of them live in trees. They have a toe at the back of their feet which helps them to grip the branches.

The perching birds are all different colours and sizes. They include the little brown wrens and sparrows and the beautiful birds of paradise. There are oven birds, lyre birds, larks, swallows, orioles, tits, thrushes, robins, waxwings and crows. The crows are very large birds. They build big, untidy nests high in the trees. The look-out post at the top of a ship's mast is called the crow's nest because it is so high up.

The perching birds are the only birds which can really 'sing'. You can often tell a bird by its song. The blackbird and the nightingale have beautiful voices. Birds use their song to call to their mates, to frighten away enemies and to warn other birds of danger. Starlings are very noisy birds. They often fight each other for food.

Golden eagle

Common nighthawk

Osprey

Birds of prey

Eagles, falcons, owls, hawks and vultures are all birds of prey. They have sharp, hooked beaks for tearing flesh and strong talons for gripping their prey.

Barn owl

Fantail pigeon

Pigeons and doves

Pigeons and doves are often tamed by man. They can be trained to carry messages, tied to their legs. The Roman Emperor Caesar used them to let Rome know about his battles in Gaul.

Great horned owl

Game birds

The game birds are hunted by man for food. They include turkeys, chickens, pheasants, partridges and grouse.

Great bustard

Rock dove

Golden pheasant

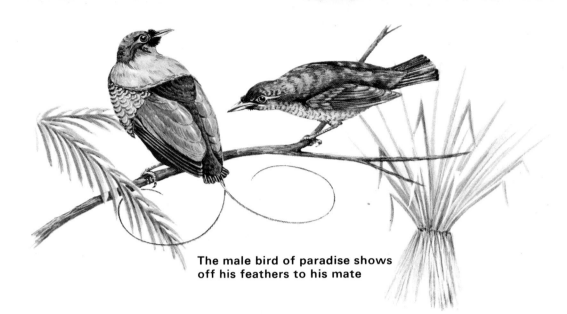

The male bird of paradise shows off his feathers to his mate

Masked lovebird

Great black cockatoo

Mynah

Tropical birds

The tropical rain forests are dark, wet places. But in the tops of the tall trees there are many beautiful birds. There are parrots, toucans, rollers, trogons and birds of paradise.

At nesting time, the male birds of paradise show off their feathers to the females, who look quite dull by their sides. The females build the nests and look after the young chicks.

The toucans have huge, brightly coloured bills. But they do not really need them because they live on soft fruits.

Cage birds

The parrot family includes parrots, macaws, parakeets, lorikeets, lovebirds, cockatoos and budgerigars. Many of these beautiful birds are kept as pets. They are very friendly and enjoy copying the sounds they hear. Many people think they can understand the words they say but they cannot really. The pretty little canaries are also kept as pets. They belong to the finch family. Mynah birds belong to the starling family. They are very good 'talkers'.

Ostrich

Kiwi

Flightless birds

Some birds cannot fly. Their wings are too small for their bodies. The kiwi lives in New Zealand. It hides in a burrow during the day and goes out to find food at night. Ostriches are the largest birds. They cannot fly but they can run very fast. Rheas and emus are also flightless birds.

Extinct birds

The dodo was a big flightless bird. There are no dodos left alive now. They are extinct. They were hunted by sailors for food. The moa was the tallest bird that ever lived. It was twice as tall as a man. It lived in New Zealand but it is now extinct.

Dodo

Bird Table

If you want lots of birds to come to your garden you can make a bird table for them. Put out some water and food. Birds love breadcrumbs, nuts and seeds. Do not give them anything salty. It will make them very thirsty and may even kill them. If you have a tree in your garden you can also have a bird box for birds to nest in.

Mammals

Mammals are the most important animals in the world. They are stronger and cleverer than other kinds of animal. The most important mammal of all is man.

It is easy to tell mammals from other animals. They always have hair or fur. Men and elephants do not have much hair, but rabbits are very furry. All mammals also feed their babies on milk.

Flying mammals

Bats are the only mammals that can fly. They have large wings made of skin. The wings stretch from their sides along their arms and long fingers. Bats sleep during the day and hunt at night. They often sleep upside down with their wings folded. Some other mammals, such as flying opossums and flying squirrels, can glide. They do not have wings which they can flap, like the bats. They can only glide from tree to tree.

Bats are the only flying mammals. Their wings are made of skin

Rodents

Nearly half the world's mammals are rodents. Most of them are small, furry animals, such as mice, rats and hamsters. Porcupines are also rodents, but they are covered with prickly spines.

All rodents have large front teeth, which are very sharp. Squirrels gnaw through nuts with their teeth. Beavers can gnaw through thick trees. Their teeth are always being worn down but they never stop growing. The largest rodent is the capybara. It is about three feet high.

Rabbits and hares

There is not much difference between rabbits and hares. They both have long ears and long back legs. Hares are slightly larger and move by jumping. Rabbits move by running.

Squirrel

Beaver

Rodents have strong front teeth that never stop growing

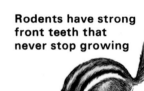

Chipmunk

Hare

Harvest mice

Rabbit

The meat-eaters

This is the best known group of mammals. It includes lions, tigers, bears and hyenas. Most meat-eating animals are hunters, but some meat-eaters, such as pandas, mostly eat vegetables. The meat-eaters are divided into seven main families. These are the cats, hyenas, civets, dogs, weasels, raccoons and bears.

Cats

Pet cats, lions, tigers and leopards all belong to the same family. They are all good hunters. They have strong claws which they can put out when they are fighting or climbing. They draw them in when they are resting or walking.

Cats are found in most parts of the world. Most lions live in Africa. They like sandy or rocky places. They live in family groups called 'prides'. Lions are very lazy animals. They sleep for most of the day and hunt at night.

Leopard cat

Wild cat

The lynx lives in parts of North America and Europe. The black tufts on its ears make it easy to tell from other cats.

Cheetahs live on the open plains of Africa. They can run as fast as motor cars. They are very good hunters.

The tiger is the largest and most powerful cat. Tigers live in India and other parts of Asia. There are no tigers in Africa. Some tigers are man-eaters. They are very fierce.

Lynx

A pride of lions. The lioness looks after the cubs and hunts for the food

Hyena

Hyenas

Hyenas live in Africa and in Asia. They often eat dead or young animals. Hyenas hunt in large packs. They have a nasty smell. When hyenas bark, they sound like people laughing.

Civets

The African civet is about the size of a dog. It has a small head and a bushy tail. A liquid from civets is used to make expensive perfume.

The mongoose is related to the civet. Mongooses are very good at killing snakes.

Mongoose

Red fox and cubs

Dogs

The dog family includes pet dogs, foxes, wolves and jackals. The fiercest hunter is the wolf. Once, wolves were found in many countries. Now they only live in the cold northern countries. Jackals live in Africa. They look like foxes. Jackals often follow hunting lions. They eat the food the lions leave.

Pet dogs are descended from wolves. Men first tamed them thousands of years ago. Wild dogs, called dingos, are still found in Australia.

Skunk

Weasels

Weasels, stoats, badgers, otters and skunks all belong to the same family. They mostly hunt small animals such as rats. Otters live in rivers and catch fish. Some stoats turn white in winter for protection. Skunks protect themselves by making a horrible smell.

Otter

Raccoon

Raccoons

Raccoons are very common in America. They eat fruit and plants as well as meat. In many American towns raccoons live on food left in dustbins. In South America there is a raccoon which catches crabs with its long fingers. The crabs do not have time to bite.

Lesser panda

Giant panda

Pandas

There are only a few pandas in the world. They live only in certain mountains in Asia. The lesser panda is smaller than the giant panda. It looks like its relative the raccoon. It lives in holes in trees. The giant panda looks like a black and white bear. It lives in bamboo forests in China. It eats bamboo shoots mainly.

Bears

Bears are large furry animals. They are closely related to the dogs. Bears can walk on two legs or on four. When a brown bear stands on two legs, it is about ten feet tall. Bears are very strong. They can easily kill a man. Most bears eat almost any meat or vegetables. Their favourite foods are fish and honey. The sloth bear has a special long mouth. It uses its mouth to dig out and eat insects. Most bears live in hills or mountains. The polar bear lives in the Arctic. It is a very good swimmer. Polar bears hunt seals.

Brown bears

Mammals with hooves

Cats and dogs have paws. Monkeys have fingers. But many animals, such as cows and horses, have hooves. The hoofed mammals are divided into two groups. Some have an odd number of toes. Others have an even number.

The horse family includes horses, asses and zebras. There are still a few wild asses, but most horses are tame. Tame asses are called donkeys. Zebras are wild animals. They live in large herds in Africa.

Rhinoceroses look very fierce, but they only eat grass. They are very well protected by their tough skins and horns. Indian rhinos have one horn. African rhinos have two horns.

Tapirs have short trunks. Most tapirs are very shy but they have a terrible bite. They live in forests in Asia and in America.

Tapir

Ass

Goat

Red deer stags fighting

Hippopotamus

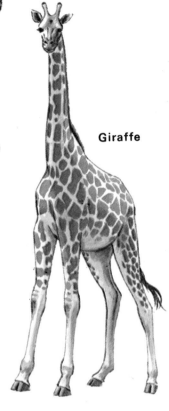

Giraffe

All hoofed mammals eat plants. Cows and antelopes eat the grass in fields and plains. Sheep and goats eat plants that grow on hillsides. Giraffes eat the leaves that grow on tall trees.

Most hoofed mammals need to protect themselves against the fierce meat-eaters. Many of them can run very fast. Some, like deer and bison, have horns or antlers. The hippopotamus is so large that it does not need much protection.

Many of these animals have been tamed by man. Cows, pigs and sheep are kept for food. Camels, llamas and yaks are used for carrying things.

Bactrian camel

Hyrax

The hyrax is a small furry animal. It lives in Africa and Asia. Hyraxes look like rabbits with short ears but they are related to elephants. Hyraxes are fierce little animals. They have sharp teeth and a claw on their hind toes. They use the claw to comb their fur.

Hyrax

Aardvark

The aardvark is a very strange animal. It lives in Africa. Aardvarks eat insects called termites. They break into termite nests with their strong claws. They dig out the termites with their long snouts. Their snouts are so tough that they do not feel the termites biting.

Aardvark

Elephants

Elephants are the largest land animals. They live on the grasslands of Africa and India. African elephants are larger than Indian elephants. It is easy to tell them apart because African elephants have much larger ears than Indian ones. Elephants eat leaves, fruit and grass. They pick food with the end of their trunks and carry it to their mouths. They also squirt water through their trunks. Baby elephants love a shower from their mother's trunk. In India, people ride on elephants. Tame elephants are also used to move heavy logs.

African elephant

Mammals that live in the sea

A few mammals live in the sea. These include whales, seals, walruses and sea cows. They cannot live under the sea all the time. They have to come to the surface to breathe. Whales can stay underwater for about half an hour.

Whales

Although whales breathe air like land animals, they cannot stay out of the water because their bodies are too heavy. Many big whales eat plankton. The killer whale eats seals, penguins and dolphins. Dolphins and porpoises are small whales. They are very intelligent.

Seals

Seals, sea lions and walruses are all members of the same family. They do not have legs like most mammals. Instead they have flippers. Seals can swim very fast, but they find it hard to move on land. Sea lions and walruses find it easier to move on land. They can lean on their large front flippers. Seals, sea lions and walruses mostly live in the sea. They hunt fish. But their babies are always born on land. Most of these animals live in cold waters. They all have a layer of fat, called blubber, which keeps them warm. Many seals live where the sea is frozen. They make holes in the ice so that they can come up for air.

Elephant seal
and cub

Manatee

Sea Cows

Sea cows are strange animals. They live in the sea and eat the sea plants. There are two kinds of sea cow. Manatees live around Africa and America. Dugongs live in the Indian Ocean.

Alaska fur seals

Duck-billed platypus

Egg-laying mammals

These strange mammals lay eggs, like the birds and reptiles. When the eggs hatch, the babies feed on milk. There are two main kinds of egg-laying mammals. Spiny anteaters live in New Guinea. Platypuses live in Australia. The platypus has fur and webbed feet with claws. It has a bill like a duck's. It makes a burrow in a river bank.

Marsupials

Kangaroos, koala bears and opossums are marsupials. Marsupials carry their babies in pouches. When the babies are born they are very small. They crawl into their mother's pouch. In the pouch the babies feed on their mother's milk. They stay in the pouch until they are quite large.

Once there were marsupials all over the world. Now most of the marsupials live in Australia. There are also a few in America.

Many marsupials look like other mammals. The pouched mouse looks like an ordinary mouse and there are even pouched cats and pouched wolves.

Kangaroo

The kangaroo is the largest marsupial. It does not look like any other mammal. Kangaroos live on the plains of Australia. They have long back legs and a strong tail. They move by jumping. Kangaroos can jump as high as five feet or more. Wallabies look like kangaroos but they are smaller. Kangaroos and wallabies eat grass.

Koala bears live in eucalyptus trees. They look just like teddy bears. Mother koalas often carry their babies on their backs. Koalas only eat the leaves and bark of the eucalyptus tree.

Koala bears

Spotted cuscus

Opossums are marsupials that do not live in Australia. They live in America. They are about the size of rats and they have tails which can grasp the branches of the trees in which they live.

The cuscus lives in trees in Australia. It hunts at night. It has big eyes to see in the dark. Wombats are only found in Australia. They dig long tunnels in the ground. They eat grass. Some marsupials are meat-eaters. Pouched wolves and Tasmanian devils are very fierce hunters.

Woolly
opossum

Insect-eaters

Hedgehogs, moles and shrews are insect-eaters but many of them eat eggs, roots and shoots as well as insects. The mole has strong claws to help it dig the long tunnels in which it lives. The hedgehog eats insects and slugs. It also likes bread and milk if some is left out for it.

Hedgehog

Mole

The little mouse-like shrews need a lot of food. In one day a shrew can eat three times its own weight in food. Some shrews die of hunger if they do not eat every two or three hours.

Pangolins

Pangolins are also called scaly anteaters. Their bodies are covered in overlapping scales and they have long, sticky tongues like the anteaters. The giant pangolin is very strong. It is almost impossible to uncurl it once it has rolled into a ball. Many pangolins live in trees. They grip the branches with their long tails.

Pangolin

Left-over mammals

The armadillos, sloths and anteaters do not fit into any of the groups of mammals. They are often called left-over mammals. Their Latin name means 'without teeth' even though the armadillo has more teeth than any other mammal.

Sloths

The sloths are very lazy and they move very slowly. They spend most of their time hanging upside down in the trees.

Anteaters

Anteaters have long claws to rip open the hard nests of termites. They lick up the ants with their long, sticky tongues. When they fight, they stand on their back legs and lash out with their claws.

Armadillos

Armadillos have a suit of jointed armour. The bands of armour on their backs are separated by soft, hairy skin. The giant armadillo is quite big but the little fairy armadillo is only six inches long. Its armour is bright pink and its hair is silver.

Anteater

Three-toed sloth

Nine-banded armadillo

Monkeys and apes

Monkeys and apes are primates. So are people. The primates are divided into four different groups. They are the prosimians, the New World monkeys, the Old World monkeys and the apes.

Prosimians

Prosimians are rather like the primates that lived millions of years ago. The tree shrew looks like a squirrel. It builds a nest in a tree for its babies. Pottos, lorises and bushbabies also live in the trees. Lemurs live only on the island of Madagascar. The indri is a lemur. It looks as if it is wearing big, woolly gloves.

Old World monkeys

These monkeys live in Africa and South-East Asia. The langurs, colobus monkeys and the funny-looking proboscis monkey feed on leaves. Guenons and mangabeys eat fruit. Mandrills and baboons live in family groups, called troupes.

New World monkeys

Spider monkeys, marmosets, sakis, and howlers live in the forests of South and Central America. Many of them can hang from the branches by their tails. At night, the squirrel monkey wraps itself in its tail to keep warm.

Apes

Gibbons, chimpanzees, gorillas and orang-utans are apes. They are man's closest relatives. The gorilla is often as tall as a man. It looks fierce but it is really very shy. Chimpanzees are smaller. They are very noisy and playful.

98

Tree shrew

Indri

Squirrel monkey

Orang-utan

Mangabeys

Mandrill

Proboscis monkey

Chimpanzee

Gorilla

99

Polar bear

Walrus

Leopard seal cub

Adèlie penguins
make a nest of
stones

Life in the Polar Regions

The polar regions are the coldest places in the world. The Arctic is at the top of the world and the Antarctic is at the bottom.

In winter, the Arctic is frozen. The polar bear roams over the ice. It has rough paws to stop it slipping. A polar bear will eat almost anything it can find but it will not attack a walrus. The walrus is a bad-tempered animal. Its long tusks frighten other animals away. Polar bears like to eat seals. Seals spend most of their time in the sea. The fiercest seal is the sea-leopard. It lives in the Antarctic and eats penguins.

Slowly the Arctic winter melts away. In summer, the ground is covered with a carpet of mosses and small plants. The ptarmigan loses its white, winter coat. Its feathers become brown to match the summer colours.

When the warmer weather comes many small animals wake up from their winter sleep. Many of the animals that spend the winter in the south return to the Arctic. Herds of reindeer arrive to graze on the plants. Ducks and geese and other birds fly back from the south. The musk ox comes down from the highlands where it has spent the winter. It sheds some of its shaggy coat in summer.

Only a few birds and seals live in the Antarctic. There is no food on land so they have to find food in the sea. The penguins only stay on land to hatch their eggs. Adèlie penguins make nests out of stones. The male penguin offers stones to the female penguin. If she takes them, they will build a nest of stones together.

Reindeer

In summer the musk ox and the reindeer graze on the Arctic plants

Musk oxen

Life in the Northern Forests

Thousands of years ago, one great forest covered most of Europe and North America. Today, there are only a few great forests in the north. The rest have been cut down to make way for roads, towns and farms.

In the north, near the Arctic, there are coniferous forests of pine, fir and spruce. Further south it is warmer. There are deciduous forests of oak, ash, elm, beech, birch and maple.

Deep in the forest there are many animals. Squirrels leap from branch to branch. They build nests called dreys. In the autumn they collect nuts and other food to eat during the long, cold winter.

The king of the forest is the moose. It is as tall as a man and it has great antlers that branch like the trees themselves.

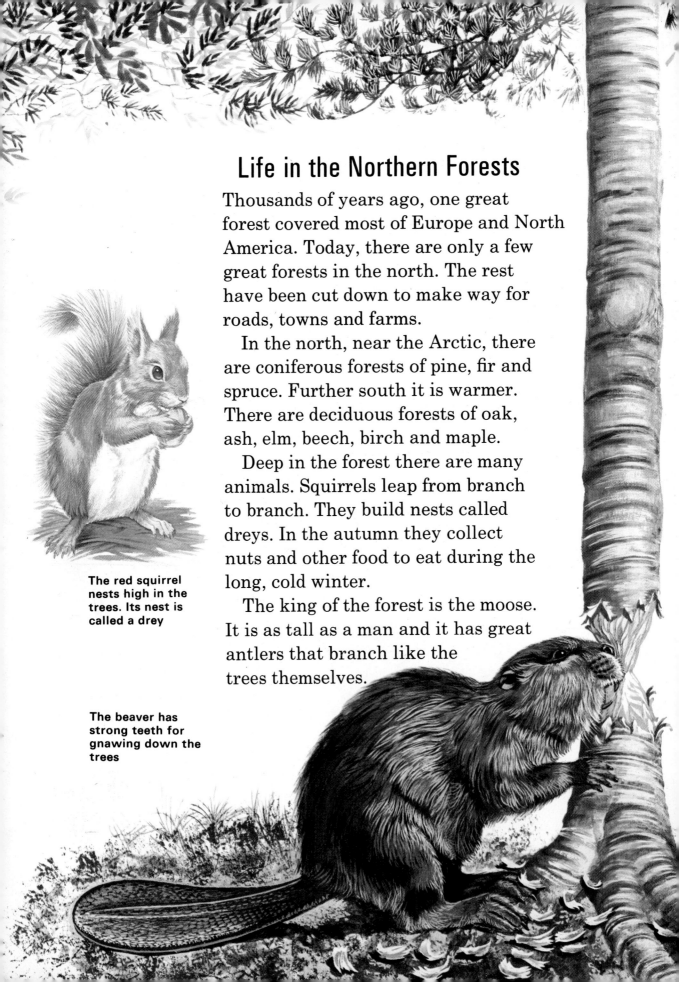

The red squirrel nests high in the trees. Its nest is called a drey

The beaver has strong teeth for gnawing down the trees

The strongest and fiercest animals in the forest are the wolves and bears. Wolves hunt in 'packs'. They can even kill a moose. Bears are even stronger but they live mostly on berries and wild fruits. The fox is a cousin of the wolf. It hunts by night. By day it hides in its burrow, or 'earth'. Foxes are very cunning animals. It is hard to catch them.

Small creatures, such as shrews, voles and mice live on the forest floor. They have many enemies. Weasels, stoats and badgers hunt them for food. The badger hides in its underground set during the day. At night it comes out to find food. It is hard to see the badger in the moonlight because of the white stripe on its face.

Beavers are the busiest animals in the forest. They cut down trees with their strong front teeth. They use the trees to build a dam across a stream. Water collects behind the dam and makes a pond. The beaver builds its home on an island in the pond. The water round the island protects the beaver from its enemies.

Many birds live in the forest. Woodpeckers have long, strong beaks. They dig into the bark of trees to find insects.

The woodpecker digs into the bark and wood of trees with its beak. It pulls out grubs for its chicks with its long, sticky tongue

The badger lives in a set under the forest floor. It is very tidy. It often cleans out its set

Bison fighting to lead the herd

Life on the Prairies

The prairies of North America are great plains of rolling grassland. Once they were covered with tall, waving grasses. Great herds of bison and pronghorns roamed the plains, grazing on the grass. But then settlers came to North America. They cut down the grasslands to make way for their farms. They built railways across the prairies and killed millions of bison for food. Now great fields of wheat stretch for miles and cattle graze on vast ranches. There is less and less room for the wild animals.

Bison are huge beasts with great shaggy shoulders. In summer, the bulls fight each other to see which one should lead the herd. Two bulls walk slowly towards each other for the duel. They shake their heads and bellow. Then they ram each other with their horns. Often the loser of the battle goes away to live by himself while the winner takes charge of the herd.

Only a few birds of prey and game birds, such as the prairie chicken, live on the prairies. But many migrating birds stop there for rest and food on their long journey from the Arctic.

Many small animals live beneath the surface of the prairies. The burrows of the prairie dogs may stretch for miles in big underground 'towns'. Prairie dogs love playing in the warm sun. They are very friendly creatures. But they have many enemies. Eagles, owls, hawks and falcons swoop down and snatch them from their burrows. Weasels and snakes follow them into the tunnels cr lie in wait for them. Badgers and coyotes dig down to get them.

Prairie dogs love to play in the sun, but they do not stray far from their burrows. There are too many enemies about

Prairie falcon

Life on the African Plains

The great plains of Africa are the home of many large wild animals. Some parts are covered with tall grasses and dotted with trees. In other parts the soil is dry and dusty with only a few small bushes and clumps of grass.

On the African plains the lion is the king of beasts. He fears no other animal. His great strength protects him from attack.

Elephants

Vultures

Cheetah chasing springboks

Pride of lions

Impalas

Bontebok

Eland

Gnus

Zebra

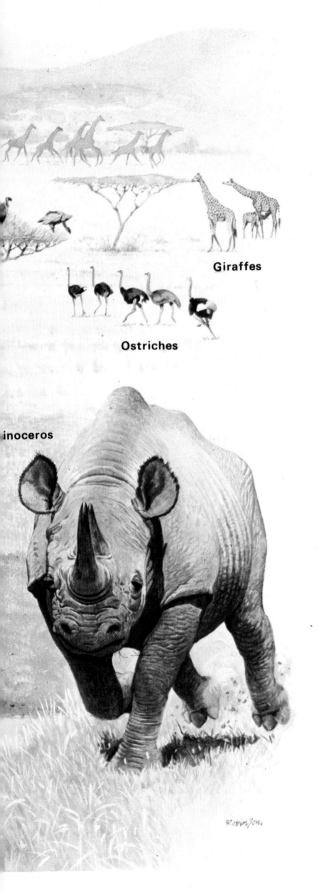

Giraffes

Ostriches

inoceros

During the day the lion is happy to lie under the trees with his family. The lioness looks after the cubs and hunts for food. She hunts at dusk, stalking and running down her prey. When the lions have eaten the vultures and hyenas move in to pick the bones.

Herds of antelopes roam over the plains. The eland is the biggest. It has long, twisted horns. The gnu looks ugly and fierce but it is really very timid. The antelopes can run very fast, but they cannot match the speed of the cheetah. It can run as fast as a motor car.

The giraffes spend most of their time eating leaves from the tops of the trees. At the first sign of danger the whole herd will gallop away.

The great elephants have nothing to fear. They move about in herds, peacefully gathering branches and grass with their long trunks.

All the animals keep away from the rhinoceros. It is a big, bad-tempered animal with a hide like armour. It cannot see very well so it charges at almost anything which moves.

Desert owl

Kangaroo rat

Bobcat

Rattlesnake

Life in the Desert

Deserts are hot, dry places where little rain falls. All day the sun beats down on the rock and sand. But at night it becomes cold. Few plants and animals can live in deserts because there is not enough water for them. But some animals and plants have learned to live in the desert. Most of the animals hide during the day to keep out of the sun.

At night, the desert is cool and quiet. But there are many animals looking for food. The kangaroo rat silently jumps from place to place, collecting seeds. The kit fox hunts the kangaroo rat. It has big ears to hear small animals moving. All of the desert animals listen for the poisonous rattlesnake. The rattle of its tail warns them to keep away. None of the animals hears the desert owl. It swoops down suddenly on the small animals it hunts.

The spadefoot toad does not like the sun. It uses its back feet to dig a hole in the ground. Then it goes to sleep. The toad only wakes up when it rains.

Spadefoot toad

The scorpion is one of the most dangerous animals in the desert. It has a poisonous sting on the end of its tail. Desert people have to be careful not to tread on a scorpion by accident.

Kit fox

The camel is a tame desert animal. It can travel for a week or more without any food or water. The camel lives on fat stored in its hump. It stores water in 'pockets' in its stomach. Camels have special pads on their feet to stop them sinking into the soft sand. The Arabian camel has one hump. The bactrian camel has two humps.

Arabian camel

The roots of a desert tree are often longer than its trunk. They go deep into the ground to find water. Cactuses store water in their thick stems. Their roots spread out to soak up any rain.

Harpy eagle

Life in the Rain Forests

In the hot lands near the equator it rains nearly every day. Big forests, called jungles, grow there. The rain makes the trees grow very fast and tall. A thick blanket of leaves grows on the tops of the trees. It is very gloomy underneath because the leaves shut out the sunlight. Not all the plants have tall stems. Some reach the sun by climbing up the trunks of the trees. Some flowers even grow in the tops of the trees. They use the remains of plants for 'soil'.

Many jungle trees have special roots. If the tree does not have strong, deep roots, the bottom of the trunk may have woody supports, called buttress roots. Some other trees are supported on 'stilt' roots which raise them off the ground.

Many animals live in the rain forests. There are birds, monkeys and snakes in the trees and insects buzzing everywhere. All the animals which live on the forest floor fear the big cats.

Toucan
Iguana
Macaw
Jaguar
Capuchin monkey
Capybara
Sloth

The leopard hunts at night. Silently it climbs a tree and waits. Then suddenly it sees its prey and pounces. Often its victim is a monkey which has come down from the tree tops.

The American monkeys spend most of their lives in the trees, swinging from branch to branch by their tails. The monkeys of Africa and Asia cannot swing by their tails. The gibbons are the acrobats of the Asian forests. They can swing by their hands or run along very, very thin branches high in the trees. They look like tightrope walkers in the circus. The lazy slow-loris sleeps all day, rolled up in a ball.

In the tops of the trees there are parrots, macaws and toucans. The American harpy eagle is a big, powerful bird. It catches other birds and even sloths in its great, hooked talons.

A gibbon balances high in the trees

Life in the Mountains

As you go up a mountain it gets colder and colder. Different plants grow at different heights. Near the bottom there are deciduous trees. Above them are the hardy conifers. Beyond the conifers only a few small plants and bushes can grow. Beyond them there are mosses and lichens. At the top of a high mountain it is too cold for anything to live.

The real mountain plants which grow on the steep, rocky slopes are called Alpine plants. They grow close to the ground and have very long roots so that the wind cannot blow them out of the soil.

Alpine plants

In spring, the Alpine ibexes fight for the females

112

Puma – the mountain lion

Only very hardy animals can live in the mountains. Wild goats and sheep wander over the high slopes in summer. They have special hooves for gripping the rocks.

The puma is called the mountain lion. It can leap from great heights on to its prey in one swift, silent spring. It hunts the little rodents that live among the rocks.

The Andean condor is a great bird. It soars high in the mountains waiting to eat any animals that have fallen down the slopes and died.

Chamois

Goat

Llama

Yak

113

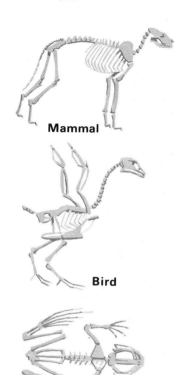

Mammal

Bird

Amphibian

Fish

How Animals Move

The skeleton

Most animals have a skeleton. Insects, crabs and snails have a skeleton on the outside of their bodies, but most animals have their skeletons on the inside. The skeleton supports and protects the body and allows it to move. Some animals which live in the water do not have skeletons. The water holds them up. But the animals that live on land have to support their own weight. They need strong, stiff bones. If we had no bones our bodies would be soft and floppy.

The hard bones protect many parts of the body, like armour. The skull protects the brain and the ribs keep the heart and lungs in a sort of cage.

The bones of the skeleton meet at joints.

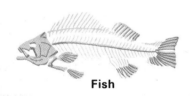

Joints, muscles and movement

The joints between the bones allow an animal to move. Different joints allow different kinds of movement. You can swing your arm round in a circle from the shoulder but you cannot bend it backward at the elbow because the joints are different.

The joints are worked by muscles. There is a muscle on each side of a joint. When you want to move your arm, your brain sends a 'message' to the muscles. One gets shorter and pulls the bone towards it. The other one gets longer so that the bone can move.

Insects have muscles inside their skeletons to move their wings. Their jointed legs are attached to the skeleton by strong muscles. Fishes have blocks of muscles all along their bodies so that they can bend them to swim. Birds have very light skeletons but the muscles that work their wings are very big. Frogs have strong leg muscles so they can jump. Most mammals run on all fours. They have many muscles to stretch and bend their legs.

With its strong leg muscles the cheetah can reach a speed of seventy miles per hour

How Animals Breathe

All animals need to breathe air. Air is a mixture of gases. The important one in breathing is oxygen. Animals need oxygen to release energy from their food. In tiny animals, such as the amoeba, air is taken in over the whole surface of the body. In most land animals it is taken in through lungs. Animals which live in the water usually have gills.

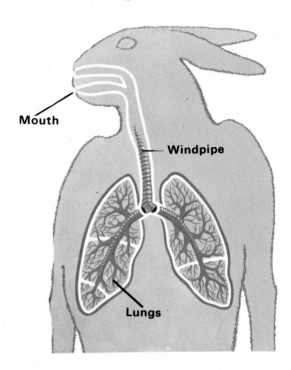

Mouth

Windpipe

Lungs

Breathing in fishes

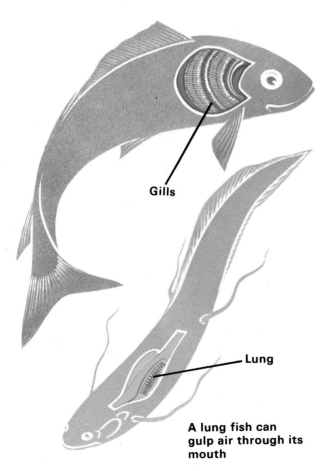

Gills

Lung

A lung fish can gulp air through its mouth

Lungs

Mammals have lungs. When we breathe, air is taken in through the nose and mouth. Little hairs in the nose trap dust and germs in the air. The air then passes down a long tube, called the wind pipe, to the lungs. The lungs are like spongy bags. Inside the lungs, oxygen passes from the air into the blood. The blood carries the oxygen to every part, or cell, of the body. Without oxygen, the body cells would die. The other gases in the air pass out of the body when we breathe out.

116

Gills

Fishes breathe through gills. The gills are connected to the mouth. The fish takes in water through its mouth and forces it over the gills. Oxygen from the water passes through the skin into the blood. The water goes out through the gill slits on the sides of the body.

Some fishes also have lungs. The African lung fish gulps air through its mouth. It can stay out of water for some time.

Other ways of breathing

Most amphibians and worms can breathe through their skins. Their skin is so thin that oxygen can pass straight through it into the blood.

Birds need a lot of oxygen. They have air sacs attached to their lungs. When the bird breathes in, lots of air passes through the lungs to the air sacs. When it breathes out, the air passes back through the lungs. Oxygen passes into the blood when the bird breathes in and when it breathes out.

Insects have a mass of breathing tubes in their bodies. The branches of the tubes reach every part of the insect's body.

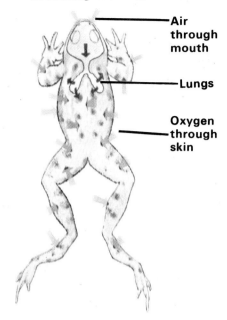

Breathing in a frog

Air through mouth

Lungs

Oxygen through skin

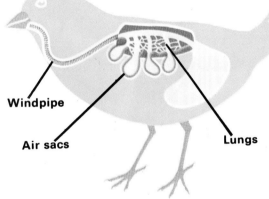

Breathing in a bird

Windpipe

Air sacs

Lungs

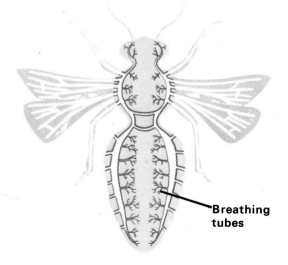

Breathing in an insect

Breathing tubes

How Animals Feed

Animals catch and eat their food in many different ways. The amoeba puts out 'arms' to catch tiny floating plants. It has no mouth or gut. Most bigger animals have mouths and a gut.

The toad has a long sticky tongue for catching flies

The caracal has long, sharp claws and teeth

Animals eat all kinds of food. Some eat only meat. They are called carnivores. Some eat only plants. They are called herbivores. Animals which eat plants and animals are called omnivores.

Carnivores

Carnivorous animals include cats, dogs, weasels, owls, snakes, frogs, sharks, ladybirds, starfishes and many other animals. Most carnivores hunt their prey and tear it to pieces with their teeth and claws. The caracal can kill a bird with one blow of its paw. Other carnivores lie in wait for their prey. Many spiders spin silken webs and snares. Some snakes and other animals use poison to kill their food before they eat it.

The langur eats only leaves. It has to eat lots and lots of leaves to get enough goodness. That is why its stomach is so big

Herbivores and omnivores

Most herbivores are peaceful animals. They include rabbits, deer, sheep, horses, snails, caterpillars and many others. Most of them feed on grass and leaves. Greenfly feed on the sap of plants. Termites and many beetles feed on wood. The elephant is the largest herbivore. It eats over half a ton of plants each week.

Omnivores eat a mixture of plant and animal food. Bears, badgers, rats and cockroaches are omnivores. So are most people.

Unusual ways of catching food

Animals use all sorts of tricks to catch their food. The chameleon shoots out its long, sticky tongue to catch insects. The archer fish shoots out a jet of water to stun insects flying above the water. The anteater has a long, thin tongue for fishing ants out of holes and cracks. The kingfisher dives into the water for fish so quickly that you can hardly see it.

Kingfishers are very good at catching minnows and other small fishes

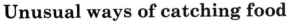

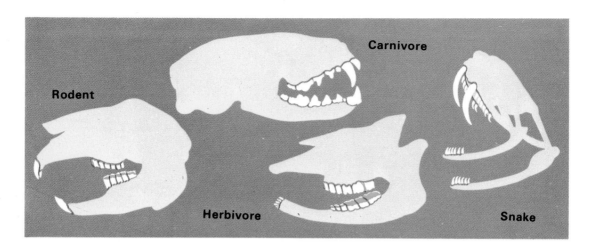

Rodent

Carnivore

Herbivore

Snake

Teeth

Many animals do not chew their food. Their simple teeth are used only to hold their prey.

Mammals have to catch, cut and chew their food. Carnivores have long eye-teeth. These stab the prey and rip the flesh. The back teeth have sharp edges to slice the meat into pieces. Grazing animals have broad, flat teeth for grinding up the grass.

Digestion

When an animal has eaten its food it must digest it. The food is digested in the gut. First, it is broken into small pieces. Then special juices break the food down into a liquid so that it can be absorbed into the blood. The blood carries the digested food to all parts of the body.

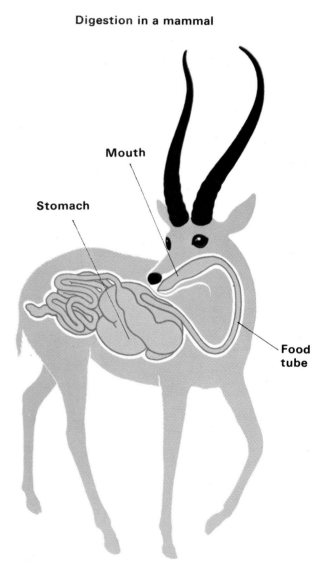

Digestion in a mammal

Mouth

Stomach

Food tube

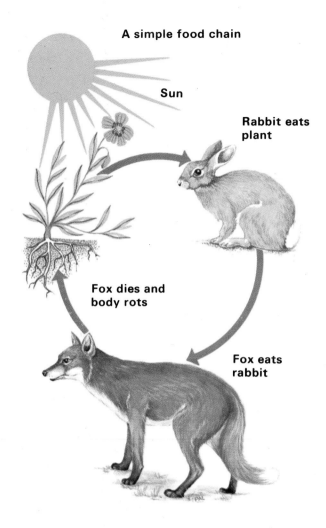

A simple food chain

Sun

Rabbit eats plant

Fox dies and body rots

Fox eats rabbit

Food chains

Green plants use the sun's energy to make food. Animals cannot do this, but they need the sun's energy. They have to get their energy by eating plants or by eating another animal which eats plants. For example, lions eat zebras and zebras eat grass. This is a 'food chain'. Some food chains are longer than this one, but every one starts with a plant. A rabbit eats a plant. It is eaten by a fox. The fox may die. Its body will rot in the soil and change into simple chemicals. The plant will take in the chemicals through its roots and the food chain will begin again.

Scavengers

Scavengers eat dead animals or animal dung. They are nature's dustmen. Some beetles and flies lay their eggs on the dead bodies of animals. The larvae feed on the rotting flesh. The scarab beetle rolls a ball of dung round its eggs. The larvae feed on the dung. Many bigger animals are also scavengers. Vultures, crows, jackals and hyenas quickly eat the flesh of a dead animal.

The scarab beetle rolls its larva in a ball of dung

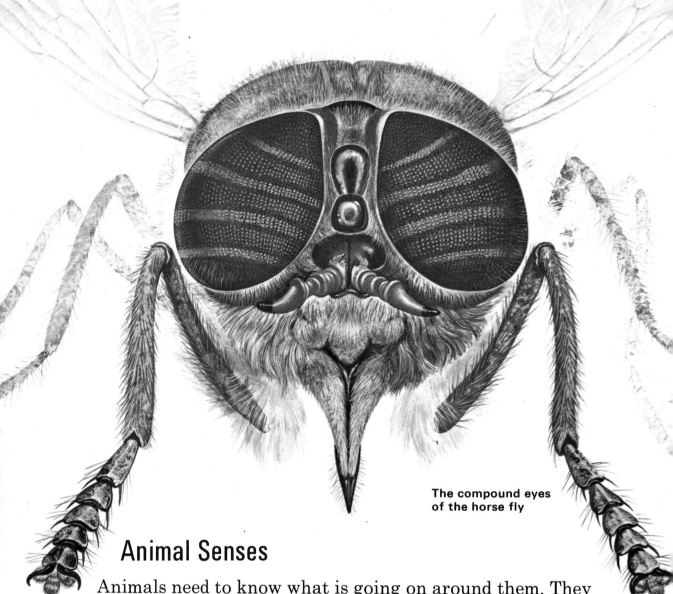

The compound eyes
of the horse fly

Animal Senses

Animals need to know what is going on around them. They use their eyes, ears and other senses to escape from danger and to find food. Simple animals, such as the amoeba, have no special senses. Their whole bodies sense danger and move away.

Other bigger animals have different senses for different uses. Many people think that they have only five senses—sight, smell, hearing, touch and taste. But there are many more. We can sense pain, heat, hunger and thirst. We also have a sense of balance.

Insects do not have the same kind of eyes as people. Their eyes are made of hundreds of cone-shaped 'lenses'. Each one works like a separate eye. Most insects also have feelers, called 'antennae'. Mice and cats have special hairs, called whiskers. They help them find their way in the dark.

Many animals rely on their sense of smell to find food and mates. Some animals can follow a scent for miles. Smell is also important to the hunted animal. It often warns him that he is in danger. A leopard stalking his prey has to make sure that the wind will not blow his scent towards the animal.

Communication

Animals cannot talk to each other as people can. But many of them have special languages of noises, signs and looks. You cannot understand the song of a robin in your garden. But it is probably saying, 'Keep out. This area belongs to me.'

When animals sense danger, they often warn their families. A rabbit thumps the ground with its back legs. A beaver slaps its tail against the water. The gorilla beats its chest.

A honeybee can tell the other bees when it has found a good patch of flowers. It does a special dance over the honeycombs. Ants 'talk' to each other by rubbing their feelers together.

The howler monkey has a bony box in its throat which makes a noise like a drum. The noise warns other animals to keep away.

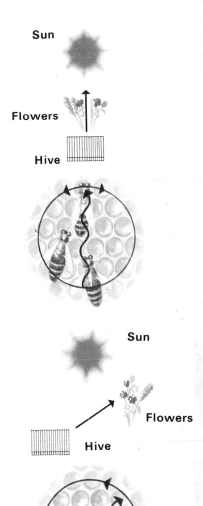

Sun

Flowers

Hive

Sun

Flowers

Hive

A bee dances over the hive. The other bees can tell where the flowers are from the dance

Howler monkeys

Courtship and Reproduction

In the breeding season, animals choose their mates. Most mammals and other animals are attracted to their mates by their smell. But some animals court their mates with special noises and displays. Birds sing, dance and show off their feathers. Usually the male bird's feathers are more colourful than the female's. The peacock displays his beautiful tail to the peahen. The pigeon puffs up his neck feathers and struts about proudly. The bowerbird builds a shelter of twigs and grass for the female. He decorates it with pretty flowers and pebbles.

Some birds and other animals give their mates presents. The male egret collects twigs and gives them to the female. If she accepts them they will build a nest together. One wolf spider wraps a tasty fly in silk and gives it to his mate. The zebra spider does a special dance to please the female. If she is not pleased, she may kill him and eat him.

The peacock displays his beautiful tail feathers to the female

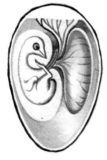

Some simple animals, such as the amoeba, reproduce themselves by splitting in two. Others such as hydra, form a 'bud' on their bodies. The little bud grows until it is almost as big as its parent. Then it breaks away to begin life on its own.

Most other animals cannot just divide or bud. Two cells have to join together before a new animal is produced. The male cells are sperms and the female cells are eggs.

When the sperm joins with the egg, it fertilizes the egg. The fertilized egg grows into a new animal.

Most amphibians, reptiles and birds lay their eggs as soon as they are fertilized. The egg contains food for the growing chick. Birds keep the eggs warm by sitting on them.

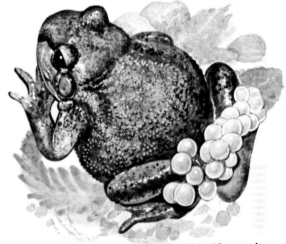

Midwife toad

The male midwife toad does not leave the eggs like most amphibians and reptiles. He carries them in a long string of jelly on his back legs.

Most mammals do not lay eggs. The young animal grows inside its mother's body. When the mother gives birth to her young, she feeds them with milk from her body.

Piglets feed on their mother's milk

Emperor penguins

Baby Animals

Many animals do not look after their young. They have to lay lots and lots of eggs because only a few of their babies will survive.

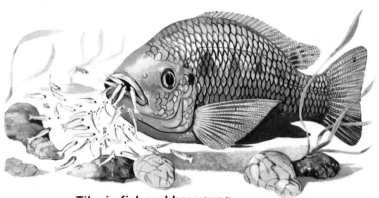

Tilapia fish and her young

It is easier for bigger animals to catch young animals and eat them if they are not protected by their parents. Millions and millions of baby fishes are eaten every year. But a few fishes do protect their young. When they are in danger, the young tilapia fishes swim into the safety of their mother's mouth.

Animals that look after their young do not lay so many eggs. The emperor penguin lays one egg. The male stands with the egg resting on his feet. His thick feathers keep the egg warm. For two months, he has no food, as he waits for the fluffy, young chick to hatch. Most mammals look after their young. They feed them and protect them from bigger animals. Some even carry them about. The baby guenon clings to its mother's stomach as she climbs through the trees.

A mother guenon and her baby

Animal Homes

Many animals are very clever builders. Most birds build wonderful nests in which to lay their eggs. Some of the most skilful builders are ants, bees and wasps. These insects live and work together in huge families. The nest of the Polistes wasp is made of lots of little 'rooms' or cells. The cells are made of paper. The wasps make the paper by chewing wood in their mouths. Bees' cells are made of wax.

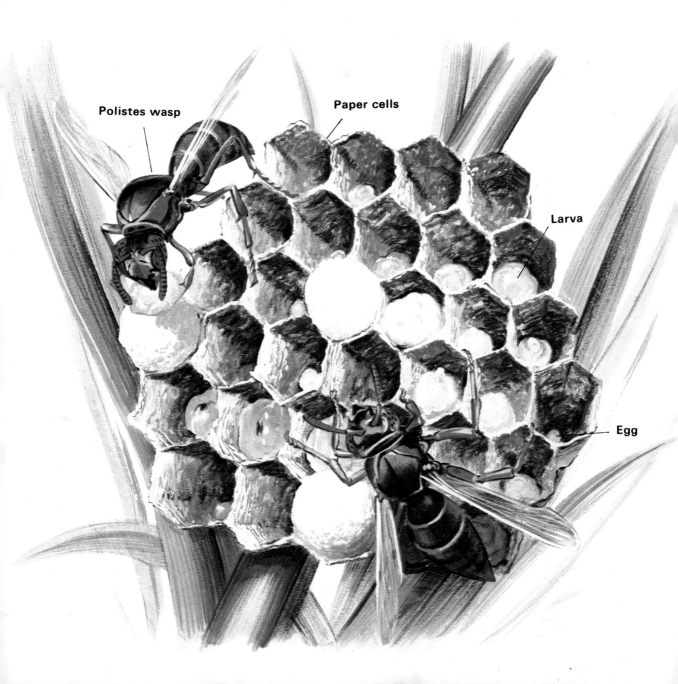

Polistes wasp

Paper cells

Larva

Egg

Elf owl

Some animals have learned to live in the hot, dry desert. The elf owl makes its nest in a cactus. It is very cool inside the cactus. The owl stays in its nest during the heat of the day. By night it goes out to hunt for food.

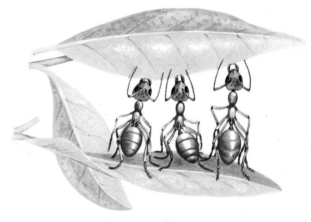

Like bees and wasps, ants live and work together. Each ant has its own special job to do. These busy weaver ants are making a nest from leaves. First the young weaver ants make silk threads. Then the workers use the threads to sew or weave the leaves firmly together. They sew with their mouths. Weaver ants live in Africa.

Weaver ants

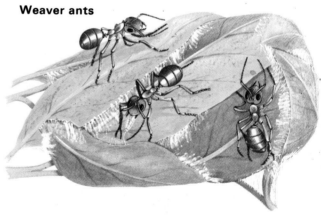

Periwinkle

Some animals carry their homes about with them. The shell of a mollusc is its skeleton and its home. The winkle's shell keeps its body moist and protects it from its enemies. The sea shells you find on the beach are the empty homes of dead molluscs.

The water spider jumps on the water and catches a bubble of air. It carries it down to its underwater home

The water spider builds its home underwater. First it makes a flat web of silk which it attaches to water weeds. Then it goes to the surface and catches bubbles of air and carries them down to the web. When the web is full of air, it looks like a dome. It is quite waterproof. The female spider lays her eggs in it.

The stickleback is one of the few fishes to make a nest. The male builds a little tunnel-shaped shelter of leaves and twigs. Then he looks for a mate. The underside of his body turns bright red. This attracts the female to share his home and lay her eggs there. The male stands guard over the nest until the eggs are hatched.

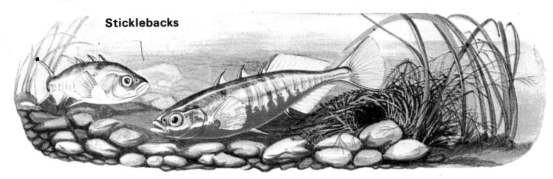

Sticklebacks

Water vole

Water voles live on the banks of rivers where there are plenty of water plants. They build burrows in the soft mud.

The beavers of North America are perhaps the cleverest of all the animal builders. They build their houses, or lodges, from wood. They get the wood by cutting down trees with their sharp front teeth. Then they cut the branches into the lengths they need for building. They usually build their lodges on the bank of a pond, or better still, on an island in the pond.

Hibernation

Many animals spend the cold winter months fast asleep. They hibernate. In the autumn, when there is plenty of food, they eat a lot and get fat. During their long winter sleep their breathing and heart-beat become very slow and they need very little food. They get the food they need from their body fat. Many small mammals, such as dormice, hedgehogs and bats, hibernate.

Many reptiles and amphibians, such as snakes, frogs and toads, also look for somewhere warm to sleep during the winter. These animals have 'cold blood'. They are as warm or as cold as the air or water around them. So when it gets cold they shelter under rocks or leaves, or burrow in the mud.

Can you see the sleeping amphibians in this picture?

The Lapps follow the reindeer herds as they migrate

Migration

Twice a year many animals, including some mammals, fishes, crabs and insects, make long and remarkable journeys. They migrate, moving from place to place as the seasons change. Birds are great travellers. Each spring, the swallow and the cuckoo leave North Africa and fly to Europe. They go south again in autumn.

Salmon and sturgeon fish migrate from the sea to the rivers and the European eel swims 3,000 miles to the Sargasso Sea to lay its eggs.

The caribou and the reindeer live near the north pole. They trek hundreds of miles south when food is short in winter. The Lapps live with the reindeer and follow them as they move.

Mallard

Golden plover

Swallow

Martin

133

The Midnight World

Many animals live in a kind of upside-down world. They sleep during the day and wake up at night. It is cooler at night and the darkness helps to protect them from their enemies. Some animals live in burrows under the ground and hardly ever come out. In the desert, most of the animals bury themselves during the day. If they did not the heat of the sun would kill them.

A barn owl swoops down to catch a mouse

The African aardvark stays close to its burrow at night. There are too many hungry animals about for it to stray far from safety

As soon as it is dark, the animals leave their homes to find food. The owl, which has slept all day in a tree, watches for rats, mice and rabbits as they scamper about. Suddenly, it sees a mouse and swoops down to seize it in its great claws.

In the woods, the hedgehog keeps a watchful eye open for the badger as it noses about for insects. When it senses danger it rolls up into a prickly ball.

Douroucoulis in their tree

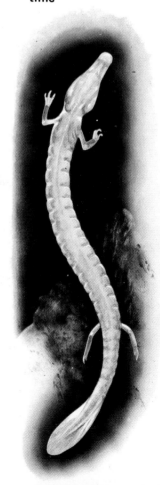

Most of the big cats go out to hunt at night. Cats can see well in the dark. Their eyes glow and the pupils go big and round. Their whiskers also help them to 'see'. Bats fly by night. They cannot see well but they never bump into things. They make noises which are reflected by objects in their path. They have big ears to hear the noises bouncing back to them. The mole hardly ever comes out of its burrow. Its eyes are weak but it has a sensitive nose to stop it bumping into things.

The douroucouli sleeps all day in a hole in a tree. But if someone taps on the tree it wakes up and looks out to see who it is.

Some creatures never see the light of day. The olm is an amphibian which lives in deep pools in caves where it is always dark. The olm is completely blind and its skin has no colour.

Animal Partners and Parasites

Some animals live together and help each other. Most of them live with other animals of their own kind. Ants build nests and work together. Deer and bison gather in herds for safety. But some animals live with quite different kinds of animals. They help and protect each other.

The hermit crab lives inside the shell of a dead sea snail. Often a sea-anemone attaches itself to the shell. It can catch lots of food as the crab carries it about. And the crab is protected by the anemone's stinging tentacles.

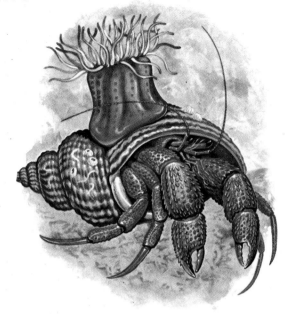

A hermit crab with its 'friend' the sea-anemone on its shell

Cattle egrets and oxpeckers rid the cattle of pests and enjoy a tasty meal themselves

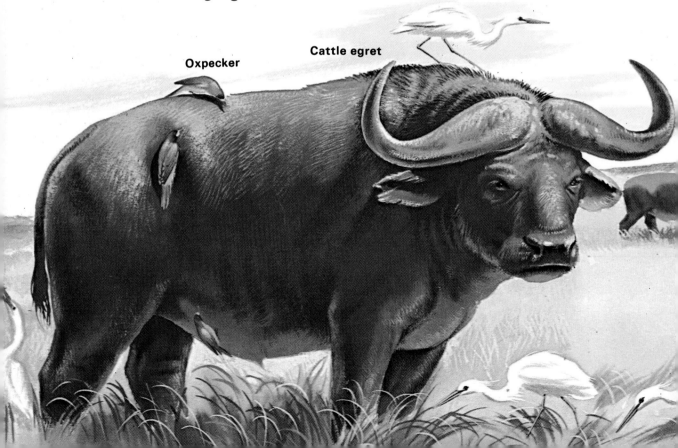

Cattle egret

Oxpecker

Coral fishes live among the stinging tentacles of a jellyfish. The tentacles protect the coral fishes from their enemies. Barber fishes live with other fishes. They eat parasites living on their scales and gills. Sometimes they even swim into a fish's mouth and eat the food stuck between its teeth.

Oxpeckers and cattle egrets live with the herds of big game animals. The oxpeckers eat ticks and other parasites living on the animals' bodies. The egrets eat the insects stirred up by the animals' hooves.

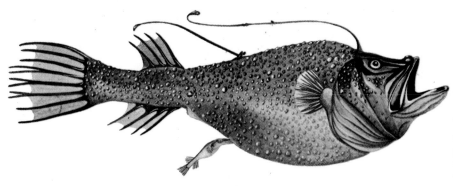

The male deep-sea angler fish is a parasite. It is attached to the female and feeds on her blood

Parasites

Parasites live on another animal but give nothing in return. Many of them are very harmful. Some spread dangerous diseases. The animal they live on is called the host.

Liver-flukes live inside the bodies of sheep and other animals. They do a lot of damage to the sheep's liver. The tapeworm lives inside the gut of its host. It eats the digested food and the host becomes thin and ill.

Fleas, lice and ticks are also parasites. Fleas pierce their host's skin and suck up its blood. Lice feed on skin, hair and dried blood.

The male deep-sea angler-fish is a parasite. It spends all its life attached to the large female by its mouth. It feeds on her blood.

The flea has no wings but it can hop from place to place, feeding on the blood of other animals

How Animals Protect Themselves

All animals need to protect themselves. Some have clever ways of escaping from their enemies.

Cinnabar moth

Warning colour

Many dangerous animals are brightly coloured. The cinnabar moth and its caterpillar taste nasty. The blister beetle's body contains a stuff which causes blisters. The painted toad has sharp teeth, like daggers. Any animal which tries to eat one will remember that it is best to leave these pretty creatures alone.

Blister beetle

Painted toad

Plant mimics

Many insects and other creatures escape from danger because they look like the trees and leaves on which they live. They are mimics.

There are lots of insects in the picture opposite. Can you see them? The diagram will show you where they are.

1. The pine beauty moth caterpillar mimics a pine needle.
2. A katydid that mimics lichens on the bark of a tree.
3. A purple thorn moth caterpillar.
4. Thorn tree hoppers mimic thorns.
5. The treble bar moth mimics tree bark.
6. The leaf bug mimic looks like a leaf.
7. A stick insect that looks like a thin twig.
8. The cossid moth mimics a flower.
9. The orchid mantis looks like a beautiful flower.
10. A giant stick insect from South America.
11. The owlet moth mimics a dead leaf.

Camouflage and colour change

The plant mimics have bodies which are shaped and coloured to look like plants. But many animals are 'hidden' by their natural colour only. They are camouflaged. The brown antelope merges with the hot, dusty plains where it lives. The tiger's stripes help it to hide in the waving grasses.

Some animals can hide in any surroundings because their colour changes to match their background. Many lizards, flatfishes, octopuses and shellfishes can change their colour.

Animal mimics

Many animals gain protection by mimicking other animals. The wasp has bright yellow stripes which warn other animals of its nasty sting. The hoverfly is harmless, but it looks so like a wasp that other animals do not attack it.

Spiders kill many small animals, but they have many enemies themselves. Not many animals eat ants because they taste nasty. So some spiders pretend to be ants. They lift up their front legs so that they look like feelers.

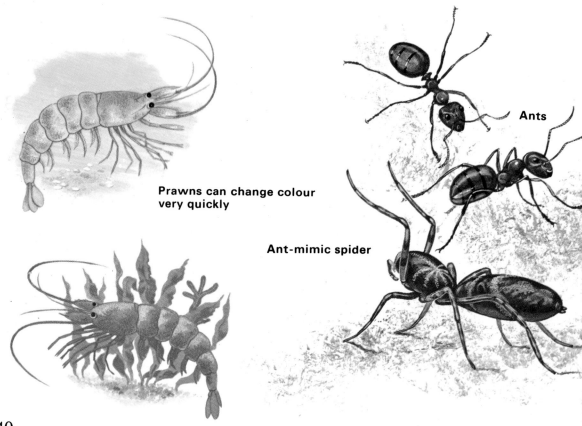

Prawns can change colour
very quickly

Ants

Ant-mimic spider

140

Armour

Many animals are so fierce that they are hardly ever attacked. But there are many peaceful creatures which need armour to protect them. Snails have hard shells to protect their soft bodies. Tortoises and terrapins also have shells to protect them. But they cannot move very fast because their shells are so heavy.

The shell of a snail or tortoise is usually in one piece. But many animals have shells made of separate parts which can be moved. Woodlice, armadillos and pangolins have 'jointed armour'. They can move quite easily and, when they are in danger, some of them can roll up into a ball.

This pangolin can roll up into a hard ball of armour

The matamata – a South American terrapin with hard points on its shell

Spines

The hedgehog has a covering of thorny spines. It can roll into a prickly ball. The porcupine has long, stiff spines on its back. It shakes its spines to warn its enemies to keep away. They make a noise like a rattlesnake. If it is attacked, it turns round fast so that its enemy hits the spines not its head.

The East African porcupine has long, stiff spines

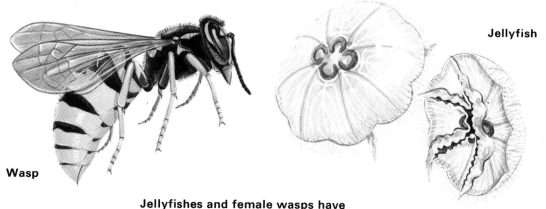

Jellyfish

Wasp

Jellyfishes and female wasps have
dangerous stings

Stings and smells

Wasps and bees defend themselves by stinging their enemies.
Wasps also use their stings when they are hunting. They sting
grubs and spiders and take them home to feed their young.
Only the female bees and wasps have stings. The honeybee's
sting has hooked barbs on the end. It pierces the skin and
poison is pumped into the wound. If its victim's skin is very
tough, the sting gets caught and the bee has to pull itself free. It
wounds itself so badly that it dies. Scorpions and jellyfishes also
have dangerous stings. When an ant is attacked it may squirt
acid at its enemy to frighten it away.

Some animals get rid of their enemies by producing a nasty
smell. Many bugs and beetles have special glands which produce
nasty smelling liquids. The skunk can spray its enemies with a
horrid smelling liquid from several feet away.

When it is in danger, the puss moth
caterpillar raises its shoulders. It makes
its head look like a frightening face.

The porcupine fish fills itself up with
water to make its spines stick out, like
armour

142

This ant raises its body and squirts acid at its attacker

The scorpion uses its sting only to defend itself

Poison and bluff

Some animals use poison to defend themselves. Many snakes are poisonous. Their fangs are long, hollow teeth. They bite their victims and inject poison into them. Some fishes have poisonous spines or flesh. They often look so fierce and ugly that they are not attacked.

Many animals fool other animals by pretending to be fiercer than they really are. The puss moth caterpillar raises the front of its body and looks very frightening. The pufferfish puffs up its body with water. Breviceps is a toad that lives in a burrow. It does not feel safe outside its burrow so it tries to look fierce by puffing up its body. When the opossum is frightened it pretends to be dead.

Breviceps is a shy burrowing toad. Its fierce look is all bluff

Poison fishes often look very ugly

143

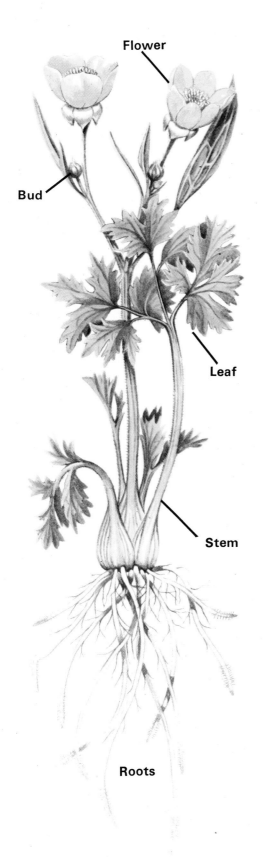

Flower

Bud

Leaf

Stem

Roots

The parts of a flowering plant

How Plants Live

Almost everywhere in the world there are plants. In the sea there are tiny, floating plants. On land there are the flowering plants. There are also many plants, such as toadstools, ferns and pine trees, which have no flowers.

Flowering plants

Most flowering plants have roots that grow down into the soil and stems that grow up into the air and towards the light. On the stems are the leaves and flowers. The young leaves and flowers are the buds. Each part of the plant does a special job.

Roots

The plant's roots keep it firmly in the ground. They stop the wind blowing it over and animals pulling it out of the ground. The roots also take in water from the soil. There are important minerals in the water.

There are two kinds of roots. One is a long, thick root, called a tap root. The plant stores food in it.

The other kind of root has many branches. It is called a fibrous root. Most garden flowers have fibrous roots. Thistles, dandelions and carrots have tap roots.

The root cap protects the root tip as it grows down into the soil. Behind the tip there are lots of tiny hairs. Water seeps into the hairs from the soil. The water then passes to the stem.

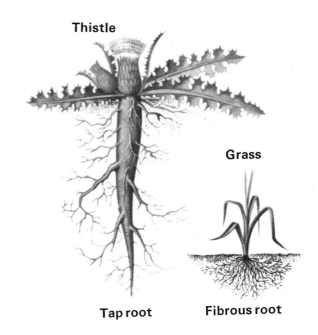

Thistle

Grass

Tap root

Fibrous root

The stem

Inside the stem of a plant, there are many tubes. The tubes carry water and food to all parts of the plant. The stem also supports the leaves and flowers. Trees need strong stems to carry all the branches and leaves.

A segment of a plant stem showing the cells

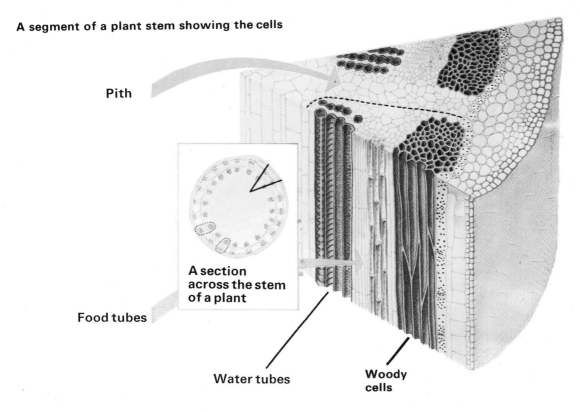

Pith

Food tubes

A section across the stem of a plant

Water tubes

Woody cells

A leaf cut through to show the cells inside

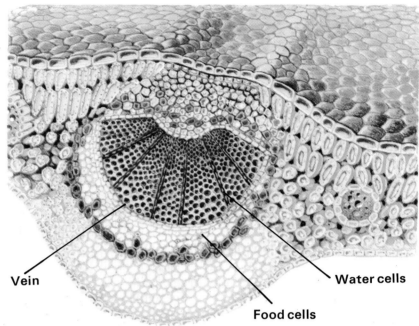

Stoma

Vein

Food cells

Water cells

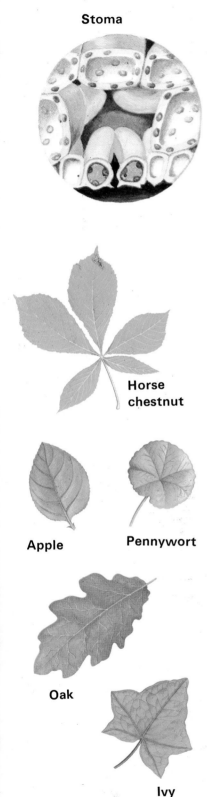

Horse chestnut

Apple

Pennywort

Oak

Ivy

Leaves

Different plants have leaves with different shapes. You can often tell a plant by the shape of its leaves.

The leaves of a plant also have tubes in them. They are joined to the tubes of the stem. The leaf is made of layers of cells. The plant makes food in its leaves and it breathes through them. The leaves have little breathing holes on the surface. They are called stomata.

How the plant makes food

To make food, plants need water and carbon dioxide. They also need sunshine. There is a special green stuff in the leaves which uses the sunshine to turn the carbon dioxide and water into food. The green stuff is called chlorophyll. The way plants make food is called photosynthesis. Photosynthesis means 'building with light'.

146

The flower

The picture at the bottom of the page is of a buttercup flower. Some of the petals have been taken away to show all the parts. On the outside there are green sepals. The sepals protect the flower when it is a young bud. A buttercup has five yellow petals. At the bottom of each petal is a part that makes sweet nectar for the insects. Inside the petals there are many stamens. Pollen is made at the top of each stamen. In the middle of the flower are the carpels. At the bottom of each carpel there is a seed-box. This is where the young seeds develop.

Some plants, such as tulips, have only one flower at the top of their stems. Some plants have more than one flower on each stem. A bluebell has several flowers hanging like bells from its stem. Other plants have clusters of flowers.

Types of flower heads

Bluebell

Tulip

Hyacinth

Ragged robin

Flowering rush

Yarrow

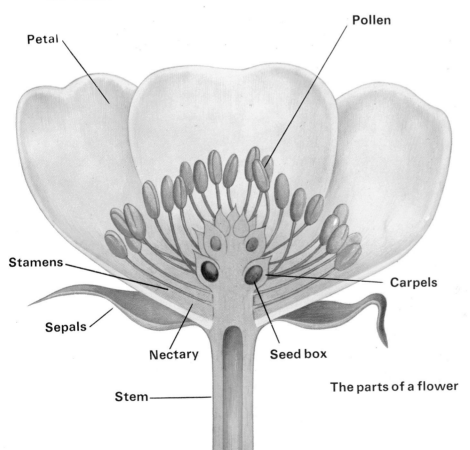

Petal

Pollen

Stamens

Carpels

Sepals

Nectary

Seed box

Stem

The parts of a flower

147

Pollination

Flowers make seeds from which new plants grow. Before a flower can make seeds it must be brushed with pollen from another flower of the same kind. This is called pollination. Most flowers cannot pollinate themselves.

A honeybee feeding on a flower

Some pollen grains magnified hundreds of times

Insect pollination

Sometimes the pollen is carried from one flower to another by insects. The insects do not mean to pollinate the flowers. They visit brightly coloured flowers to feed on the nectar at the bottom of the petals. As they reach into the flowers pollen clings to their bodies. As they move from flower to flower the pollen is brushed on to the carpels.

Hazel catkins

Wind pollination

Grasses and many trees do not have bright petals and nectar to attract insects. Their pollen is blown by the wind. Only the yellow flowers on a hazel tree make pollen. These grow in clusters, called catkins. The wind blows the pollen from the catkins.

Poppy

Buttercup

Carpels

Seeds

Blackberry

Strawberry

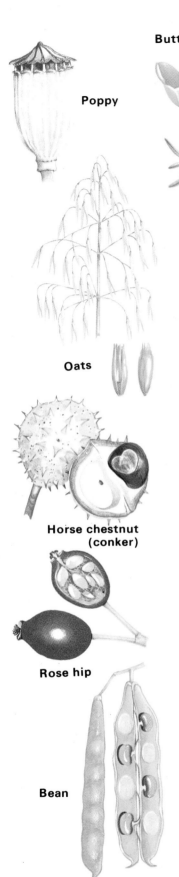

Oats

Horse chestnut (conker)

Rose hip

Bean

Seeds

When a flower has been pollinated, the seeds begin to grow in the seed-box. The seed is a tiny plant. It has a root, a shoot and one or two leaves. It is surrounded by food and it has a hard case. While the seed, or seeds, have been growing, the carpel around them has also been growing. It has become a fruit.

Fruits

Fruits come in all different shapes and sizes. Some are hard and woody. Some are soft and juicy. Some are tough and leathery.

Some fruits are not made from just the carpel. Apples and pears are formed from the flower stalk as well. The stalk swells up to form the juicy fruit. The carpels with the seeds inside them form the core inside the apple.

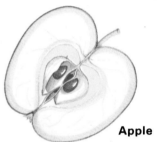

Apple

Pea

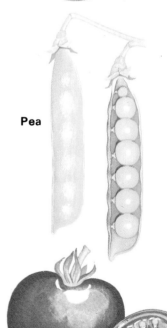

Tomato

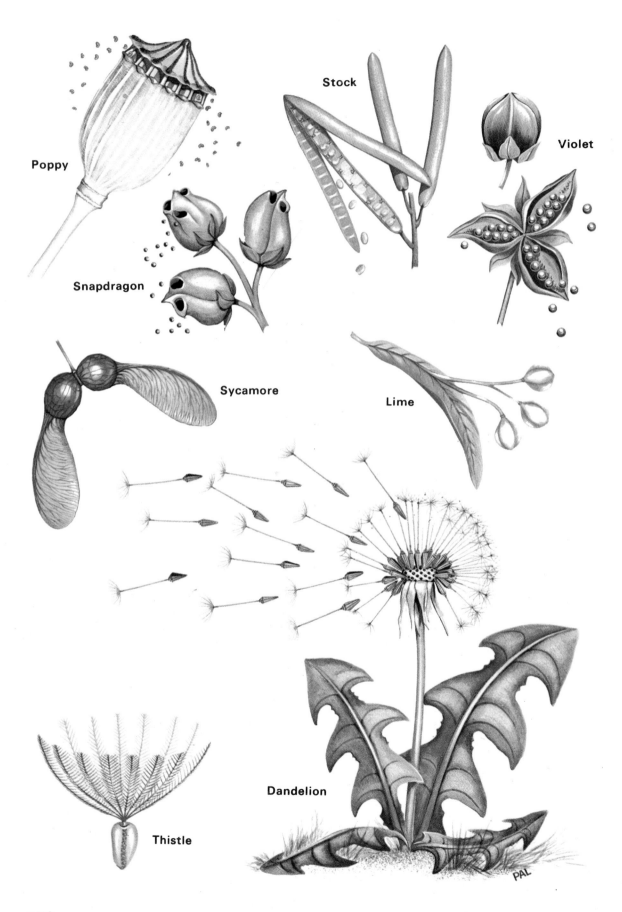

Poppy

Stock

Violet

Snapdragon

Sycamore

Lime

Thistle

Dandelion

PAL

150

Scattering fruits and seeds

When the fruits and seeds are ripe they fall from the plant. The seeds of some flowers, such as the poppy and the snapdragon are shaken from holes in the fruits by the wind. The fruits of the stock dry out as they ripen. When they are ripe the pods burst open and the seeds are flicked on to the ground.

Many seeds are scattered by the wind. Dandelion and thistle fruits have hairy parachutes. The wind carries them for miles. Sycamore and lime fruits have wings. They can glide a long way through the air.

Some fruits are carried away by animals. Birds eat mistletoe berries and squirrels eat acorns. Ants take home seeds to feed their young. Sometimes the animals drop the seeds on the ground and a new plant can grow. Prickly burrs stick to the fur of animals. They may be carried a long way before they drop to the ground.

The seeds of the water-lily and many other water plants are full of air bubbles. They float away on the water.

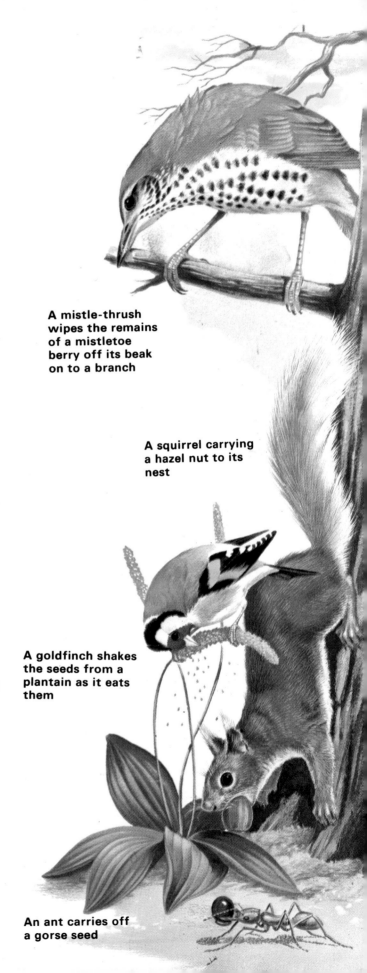

A mistle-thrush wipes the remains of a mistletoe berry off its beak on to a branch

A squirrel carrying a hazel nut to its nest

A goldfinch shakes the seeds from a plantain as it eats them

An ant carries off a gorse seed

Germination

Inside every seed is a small plant with lots of food round it. When the seed has fallen on the right ground it will begin to grow. This is called germination. The plant grows as it feeds on the food.

You can watch a bean grow if you put it between blotting paper and the side of a jam jar. You must keep the paper wet. After a few days, the hard shell of the seed splits. Out comes a small root which grows downwards. Then a small stem grows up from the seed. It has leaves at the top. The root and stem keep on growing and the root grows side roots. The plant is now a seedling and it has used up all the food in the seed.

Now it has to be put in the soil where it can get water and minerals for its leaves to make food. The bean plant lives for only one year, so it must grow very quickly and make seeds by the end of the summer. The flowers are pollinated by insects. The seeds grow and ripen in the seed pods. When the pods are ripe they can be picked and new plants can be grown from the beans.

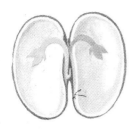

Beans in a pod

Seed

Food

It is easy to grow a bean plant in a jam jar. When the seedling has grown it must be planted in the soil

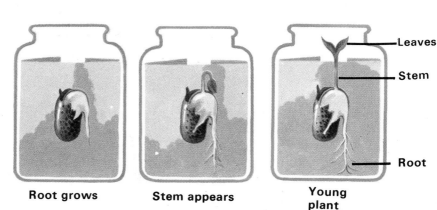

Root grows

Stem appears

Young plant

Leaves

Stem

Root

How plants store food

Many plants do not use all the food they make at once. They store some of it to use later. Carrots store food in their long tap root. The plant makes food in the spring and summer and then dies down in the winter. Next spring, it uses the food to make new leaves and flowers.

Some plants store food in their stems. Crocus corms and potatoes are swollen underground stems. Cabbages and tulips store food in their leaves. A bulb is made of special swollen leaves, packed round tiny buds. In spring, the buds use the food to grow into new leaves and flowers.

Tulip bulb

Strawberry runners

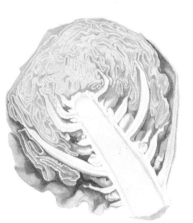

Cabbage

Vegetative reproduction

Many of the simplest plants, such as bacteria, reproduce themselves by splitting in two. Others reproduce when two cells join and seeds are formed. But some plants can also reproduce by sending out special shoots which put down new roots. The strawberry plant sends out thin stems, called runners. They grow over the surface of the ground and the tip grows roots. New leaves grow and the runner dies, leaving a new and separate plant. Some plants, such as irises and mint, put out underground stems, called rhizomes, in the same way. This is called vegetative reproduction.

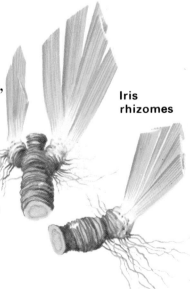

Iris rhizomes

Fungi

Most plants have green leaves and flowers. Mushrooms and toadstools are different. They are plants, but they do not have green leaves or flowers. They belong to a family of plants called fungi.

If you go out into the fields early in the morning you may see mushrooms growing in the grass. They look like little umbrellas.

Mushrooms cannot make their own food. They feed on dead leaves and wood in the soil. If you look underneath the cap of a mushroom, you will see its gills. On each gill there are thousands of spores. The spores are blown by the wind. If they land where there is plenty of food, they start to grow. They do not grow roots and shoots like green plants. The spore puts out small threads which grow branches. Some of the branches join together to make a small 'button', no bigger than the head of a pin. The little button takes in food and grows until it breaks through the surface. It grows bigger and bigger. Soon it is too big for its skin. The skin breaks and the little button cap spreads out like an umbrella. A ragged ring of skin is left on the stalk. The new mushroom quickly sheds millions of new spores.

Spore puts out thread

Threads branch

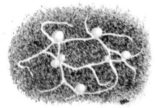

Small buttons grow

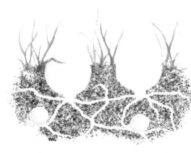

Buttons break surface

Button mushroom

Skin breaks

Mushroom with ripe spores

Horse mushroom

Boletus luridus

Oyster mushroom

Grisette

Turban fungus

Chanterelle

Cage fungus

Lactarius volemus

Clitocybe geotropa

Shaggy cap

Morel

Fly agaric

St George's mushroom

Amanita caesarea

Parasol mushroom

Wood blewit

Cup fungus

Death cap toadstool

Yellow stalk toadstool

Boletus mushroom

Moulds

Moulds are another kind of fungus. They usually grow on things that are rotting. The fluffy growth that you see on cheese or bread that has been left to go bad is mould. That is why we say that the food is mouldy. Pin mould grows on cheese and bread.

Fungi which cause plant diseases

Fungi often cause disease in plants. Ergot is a disease in rye caused by a fungus. People who eat bread made from the diseased rye become very ill. Another fungus causes potato blight. The fungus attacks the leaves of the plant and the potatoes under the soil begin to rot. Once, in Ireland, this blight ruined all the potato crops and many people starved.

Dry-rot

Dry-rot is a fungus which attacks wood and furniture in houses. The fungus eats away the wood, making floors and walls crumble. The fungus grows on damp wood and spreads very quickly.

Pin mould growing on cheese

Potato blight

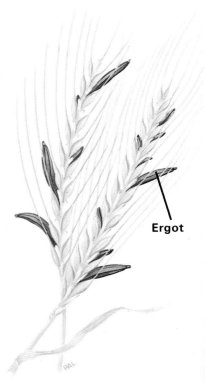

Ergot

156

Yeast

Yeast is a very useful fungus. It is used to make bread and beer. Yeast cells are very tiny. They feed on sugar and starch. As they feed, they give off a gas called carbon dioxide.

Bakers make dough for bread from flour, sugar, milk and water. There is a lot of starch in flour. If the dough were cooked it would be flat and hard. But the baker adds yeast to the dough. The yeast feeds on the sugar and starch, and gives off bubbles of carbon dioxide. These bubbles are trapped in the dough and make it rise. When the bread is cooked, it is soft and light.

Penicillin

Penicillium is another mould that sometimes grows on bread. It is made of thousands of tiny threads. A scientist called Alexander Fleming discovered that the penicillium mould could kill germs. Now the mould is specially 'grown' and made into a drug called penicillin. Penicillin is used to cure many diseases from sore throats to scarlet fever. Many people would have died without penicillin.

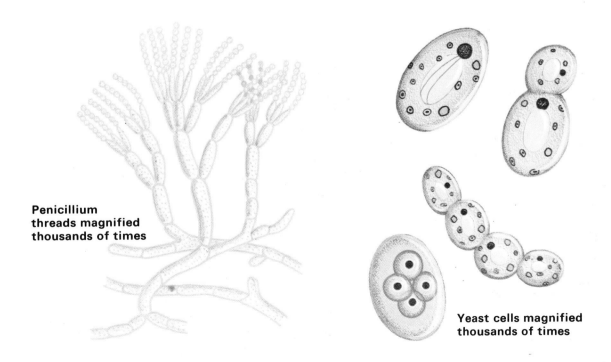

Penicillium threads magnified thousands of times

Yeast cells magnified thousands of times

Plants Without Flowers

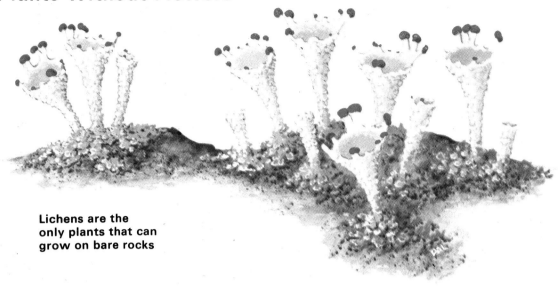

Lichens are the
only plants that can
grow on bare rocks

Lichens

Lichens are strange plants. They are not one plant but two. Part of the lichen is a fungus and part of it is a plant called an alga. The alga and the fungus live together and help each other to live. Because they help each other, lichens can grow where normal fungi cannot grow. They can grow on bare rocks where there is no food for the fungus. The algae can make food from the sunlight and from the water which the fungus stores. So the algae feed the fungus.

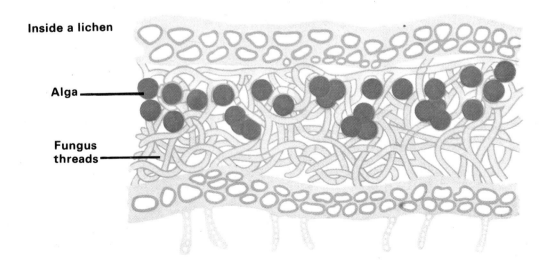

Inside a lichen

Alga

Fungus
threads

Mosses

Mosses are very simple plants. They are green and they can make their own food but they do not have flowers or seeds or proper roots. Mosses grow from spores. The fully grown moss plant puts up a stalk. On the top of the stalk is a 'box' which contains spores. The box opens in dry weather so that the wind can scatter the spores. It stays shut when it is wet. When the spore lands in the right place it sends out a green thread. The thread grows branches. Buds form on the branches and each bud grows into a new moss plant. New threads and buds can be produced at any time, so mosses often cover the ground like a carpet. Mosses grow best in moist, shady places. They like river banks and tree trunks.

Heathland moss

Hair moss

Bog moss

A flat liverwort showing the spore 'boxes'

Liverworts

Liverworts are related to the mosses. Some look like mosses but the others have flat leaves like seaweed. They can reproduce by means of buds or spores. Many of them can also reproduce by producing 'gemmae'. These are little buds that grow in 'cups' on the leaf. They are scattered by raindrops and soon grow into new plants.

Gemma cup

Ferns

Ferns and their relatives belong to a very old group of plants. Over 250 million years ago there were great forests of ferns, club mosses and horsetails. Some of them were more than 100 feet tall. Today ferns are not nearly so big.

Unlike mosses, ferns have proper roots. They have stems and leaves but none of them has flowers. Fern stems do not usually have branches. But brackens and some other ferns have branching underground rhizomes. The rhizomes spread through the soil and put up leaves all over the place.

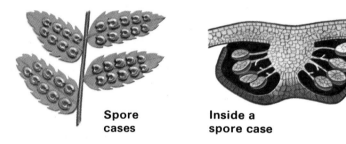

Spore cases

Inside a spore case

Ferns grow from spores. These are formed in small brown cases on the underside of the leaf or on special stems. When the cases are ripe they snap open and the spores are scattered in the wind. When the spore falls to the ground it does not grow into a new fern plant. It grows into a little heart-shaped plant, which later produces the fern.

Bladder fern

Buckler fern

Hart's tongue fern

Bracken rhizome branching

Horsetails

Ripe spores

Scale leaves

Horsetails

Horsetails are related to ferns. They are rather spiky plants. They do not have proper leaves. Some of them have branches but others have no branches at all. The stems look like pencils sticking up from the ground or water. All the way up the stem there are little 'collars'. They are tiny 'scale' leaves.

The horsetails have rhizomes like the bracken ferns. The stems die down every year but the rhizomes remain to produce the next year's stems.

The spores are produced in the little cones at the tips of the stems.

Club mosses

Club mosses are small plants that look like mosses. They grow close to the ground and their leaves are very small. But they are more closely related to ferns than to mosses. They reproduce in the same way. The spores are in 'cones' at the tips of the upright stems. The spores do not develop into club mosses. They develop into root-like tubers before a new club moss grows.

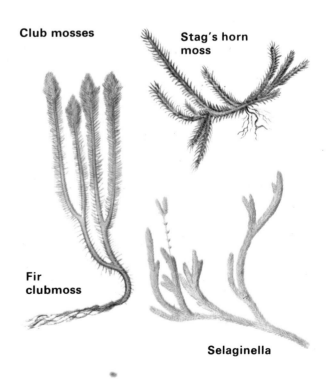

Club mosses

Stag's horn moss

Fir clubmoss

Selaginella

161

Flowers

Flowering plants are the most successful plants of all. There are over 250,000 different kinds, including grasses, bushes, trees and flowers.

The grass family includes wheat, rye, barley and all the other cereal crops.

The rose family does not just contain beautiful roses. It includes, apples, strawberries, blackberries and plums.

The pea family contains broom, clover and beans.

Cabbages are flowering plants. The cabbage family includes wallflowers, watercress and candytuft.

The largest flower family is the daisy family. It includes dandelions and thistles. The flowers are not just one flower. They are clusters of tiny flowers, called florets.

Plants from almost every wild flower family have been specially bred to produce beautiful garden flowers. But the flowering plants are not just good to look at. They provide us with food, herbs, medicines, dyes and cloth.

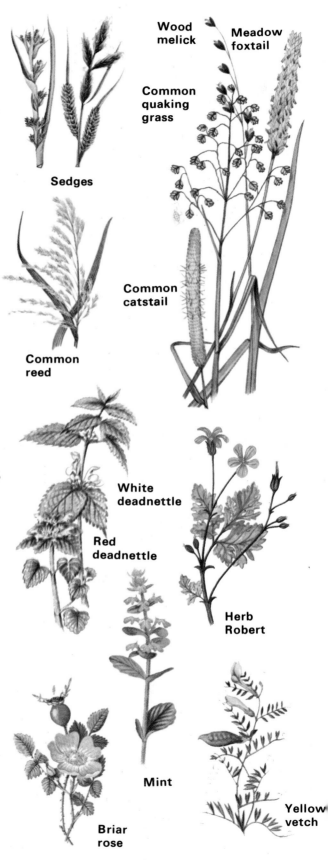

Sedges

Wood melick

Meadow foxtail

Common quaking grass

Common catstail

Common reed

White deadnettle

Red deadnettle

Herb Robert

Mint

Briar rose

Yellow vetch

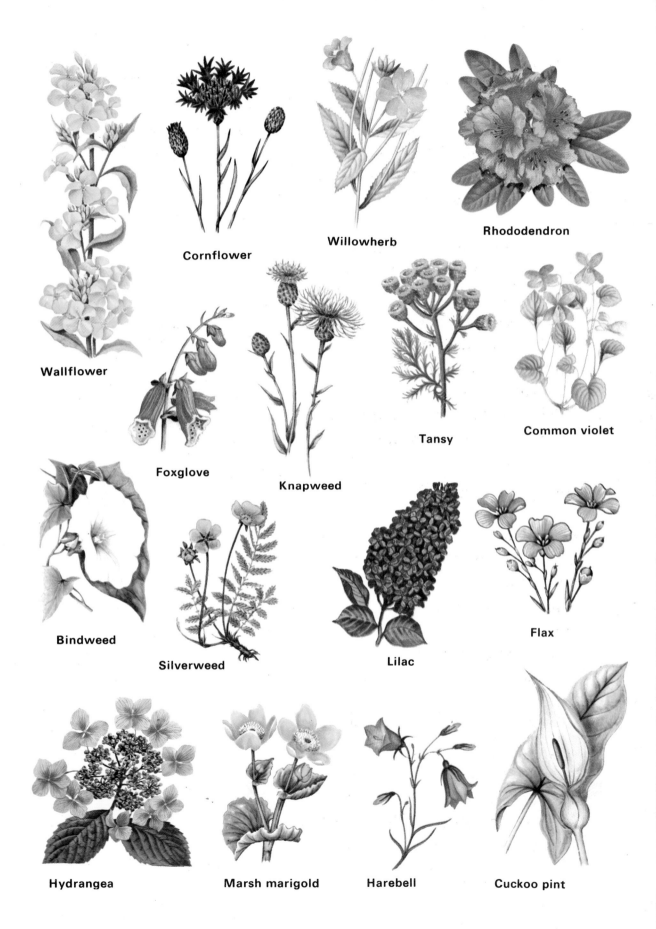

Wallflower

Cornflower

Willowherb

Rhododendron

Foxglove

Knapweed

Tansy

Common violet

Bindweed

Silverweed

Lilac

Flax

Hydrangea

Marsh marigold

Harebell

Cuckoo pint

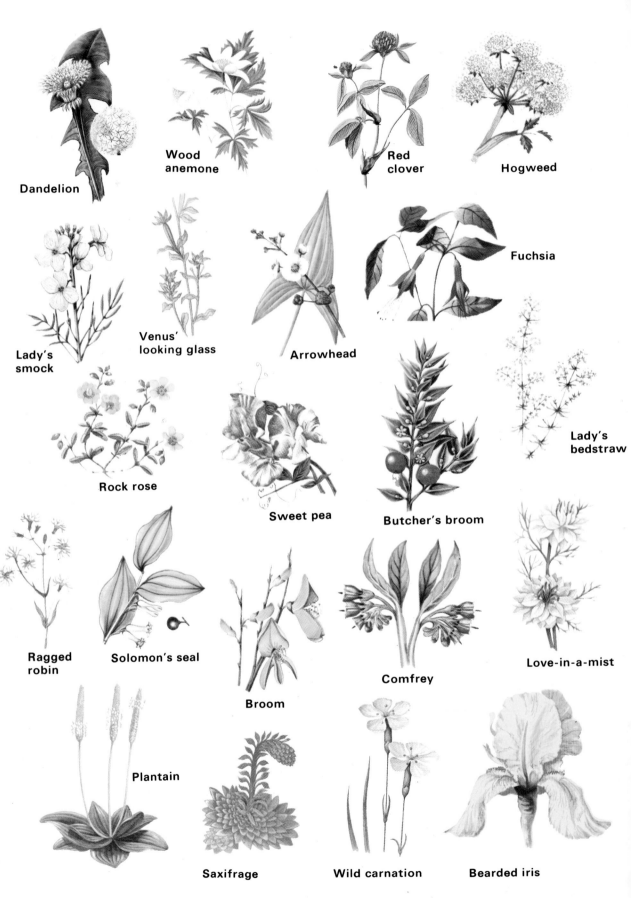

Dandelion

Wood anemone

Red clover

Hogweed

Lady's smock

Venus' looking glass

Arrowhead

Fuchsia

Rock rose

Sweet pea

Butcher's broom

Lady's bedstraw

Ragged robin

Solomon's seal

Broom

Comfrey

Love-in-a-mist

Plantain

Saxifrage

Wild carnation

Bearded iris

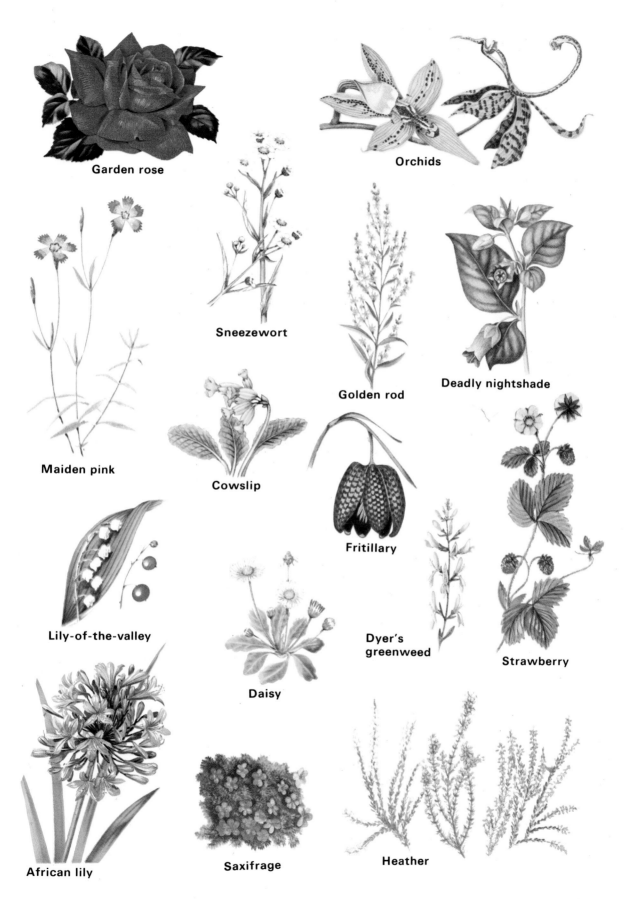

Garden rose

Orchids

Sneezewort

Golden rod

Deadly nightshade

Maiden pink

Cowslip

Fritillary

Strawberry

Lily-of-the-valley

Daisy

Dyer's greenweed

African lily

Saxifrage

Heather

165

Unusual Plants

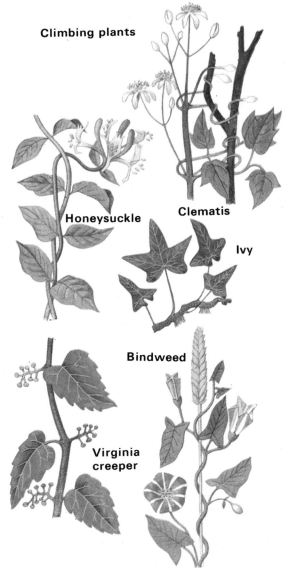

Climbing plants

Climbing plants

The tallest plants have the most chance of getting sunlight. But tall plants need strong stems and they take a long time to grow. So some plants take a short cut. They climb over other plants. Some climbing plants, such as peas, have little threads, called tendrils. These twine round anything they touch and hold the plant up. Ivy stems have little roots which give out a sticky liquid and 'glue' the plant to its support. The bindweed and the honeysuckle twine their whole stem round the stems of other plants.

Honeysuckle

Clematis

Ivy

Bindweed

Virginia creeper

The suckers of a young mistletoe plant on its host

Plant parasites

In winter, you sometimes see mistletoe growing on the branch of an apple tree. Mistletoe is a parasite. It can make food in its leaves but it has no roots of its own. So it sends suckers into the branch of a tree. The suckers take in water and minerals from the tree. Some parasites do not just 'steal' water and minerals. They take everything they need. The dodder has a long red stem. It twines round other plants and sends suckers into them. Often it kills the top part of the host plant.

Insect-eating plants

Some soils do not have enough minerals for plants to make food. So some plants get more minerals by eating insects. They trap the insects and digest their bodies. The pitcher plant is a large tropical plant. Its leaves are shaped into a sort of jug, or pitcher. Insects that land on the rim slide down the slippery surface inside the pitcher and drown in the liquid at the bottom. The sundew and the bladderwort also eat insects.

How plants protect themselves

Prickles and thorns stop animals eating plants. In dry places many plants have prickles instead of proper leaves. They do not lose as much water as leaves.

Stinging nettles have poisonous hairs. When an animal brushes against a nettle, the sharp little hairs stick into it. Poison from the hair causes the sting. The fever nettle grows in West Africa. It can make a man quite ill.

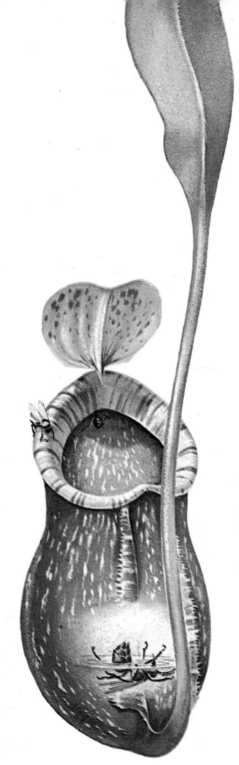

An insect is trapped in this pitcher plant. The plant can live without insects but it does not produce many flowers and seeds

167

Trees

Trees are the biggest plants in the world. They need thick, woody stems to support their weight. It takes a long time for a tree to grow big and strong. Some giant redwoods are over 300 feet tall and some of them have been growing for more than 3,000 years.

Trees are very important. They give us wood, food, paper, cork and rubber. Their wood can even be made into dress material. Because trees are so useful, many forests have been cut down. In some countries there are great deserts where the trees have been removed and not replaced. The soil has lost its moisture and there are great dust storms. Today people are more careful to plant new trees when they cut them down.

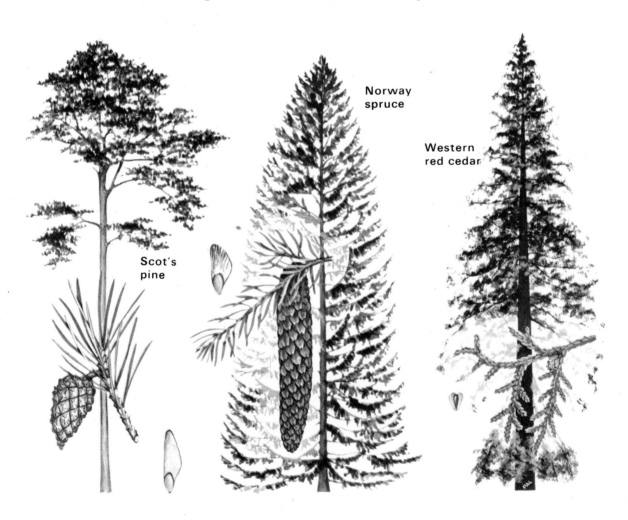

Norway spruce

Western red cedar

Scot's pine

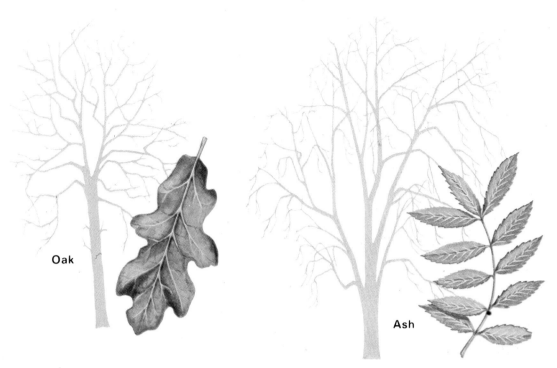

Oak

Ash

Evergreen trees

Some trees have leaves on all the year round. They are called evergreens because they always look green. Many evergreens bear their seeds in cones. They are called conifers, which means 'cone-bearers'. Most conifers have leaves like tiny needles. Their wood is quite soft and they are sometimes called 'softwoods'.

Deciduous trees

Deciduous trees drop their leaves in the autumn and grow new leaves in the spring. Most of them have broad leaves and their wood is harder than conifer wood. Sometimes they are called 'hardwoods'.

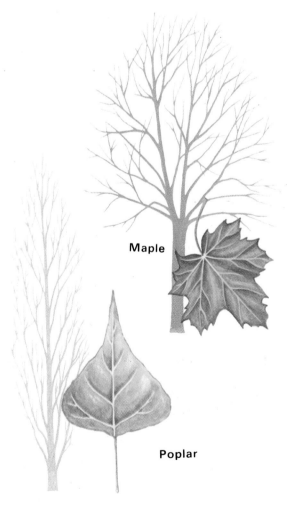

Maple

Poplar

169

Fruit

Flowers

Buds

Leaves

Branches

Trunk

Roots

Trees have the same parts as any ordinary smaller plant

Parts of a tree

Although trees are so large, they are built in the same way as any ordinary plant, like a buttercup or a rose bush.

The trunk is a woody stem which holds up the branches and the leaves. The leaves make food for the tree. The wood in the middle of the trunk is called heartwood. Around this is sapwood. Sapwood carries water up the trunk to the leaves. The bark round the trunk protects the tree.

Under the ground are the tree's roots. They have to be long and strong to anchor the tree firmly in the ground.

Palm trees and ginkgos

Palm trees do not have solid, woody stems. The tubes which carry the water are scattered through the trunk. The leaves are long and wavy. Palm trees provide food and shelter for many of the people who live in tropical lands.

The ginkgo, or maidenhair tree, has been on earth longer than any other tree. It has no real flowers and is distantly related to the conifers.

Wood

A tree's wood is made from the tubes which carry water and food in the trunk. They grow in rings round the outside under the bark. The tree grows new tubes each year. The old tubes go hard and woody. So every year the trunk of a tree gets a little thicker. In spring, the bundles of tubes are wide because the tree needs lots of water to grow new leaves and flowers. In autumn, the tubes are much narrower and the wood they make is much darker than the spring wood. These dark rings of wood are called annual rings. Each one marks the end of a year's growth. If you count the rings, you can tell how old the tree was when it was cut.

When a piece of wood is sawn from a tree, the annual rings show up as a pattern. This pattern is the grain of the wood. You can often see dark spots in wood. They are knots. Knots are the remains of the tree's branches.

Oak grain

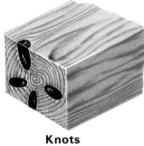

Spruce grain

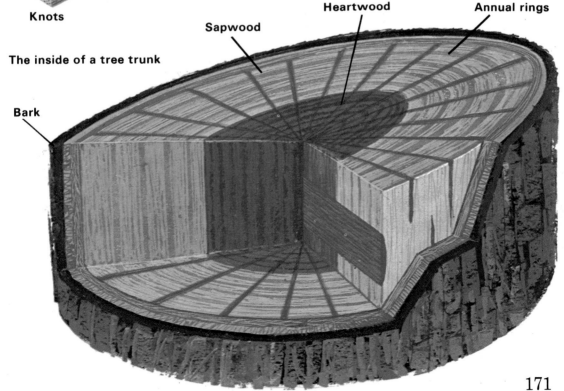

Knots

The inside of a tree trunk

Sapwood

Heartwood

Annual rings

Bark

Flowers

Conifers bear their seeds in cones but all other trees have flowers. Many of them have small, dull flowers, like the oak, ash, elm and maple. But some have beautiful flowers, like the magnolia, apple, lilac, almond and horse chestnut.

Fruits and seeds

You can often tell a tree by its fruits and seeds. The oak has little acorns in tiny cups. The seeds of cherries and pears are inside the flesh of the fruit. Some trees produce seeds which are good to eat. Walnuts and hazel nuts taste very good. Sycamore and maple fruits have wings on which they are carried through the air.

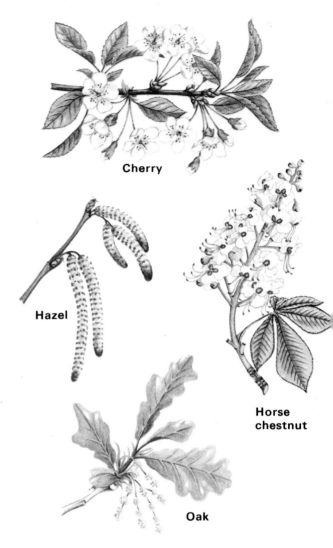

Cherry

Hazel

Horse chestnut

Oak

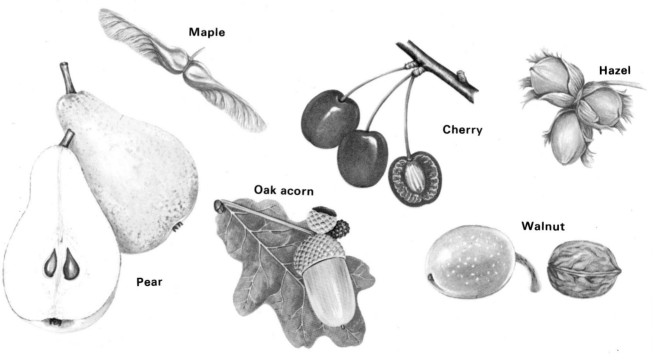

Maple

Pear

Oak acorn

Cherry

Hazel

Walnut

Cones

Pines, spruces, cedars, larches and monkey puzzle trees are conifers. The cones are made of very special kinds of leaves. These 'leaves' are the hard scales of the cone. Conifers have male and female cones. In dry weather the cones open and pollen from the male cones is blown into the female cones. The male cones then die but, inside the female cones, the seeds grow. Pine cones and seeds take two years to ripen.

Growing a forest

Every year many trees are cut down. New trees must be planted so that there will be plenty of trees in years to come. It takes about thirty years for a tree to grow. The forester plants the seeds in a nursery. After a few years the seedlings are strong enough to be planted out in the forest. They are planted close together so that they grow straight. When they are bigger the forester cuts back the lower branches and removes some of the trees to make room for the others.

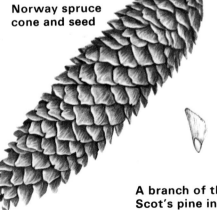

Norway spruce cone and seed

A branch of the Scot's pine in spring. The new cones are at the tips of the shoots. The cone shedding its seeds is two years old

You can usually tell a tree by its shape and its leaves. The poplar is tall and thin. The maple is big and wide. Most conifers have a single, unbranched trunk, but the leaves and cones are often very different. Some have thin needles like the Norway spruce–the Christmas tree. Others have scale-like leaves like those of the Lawson cypress.

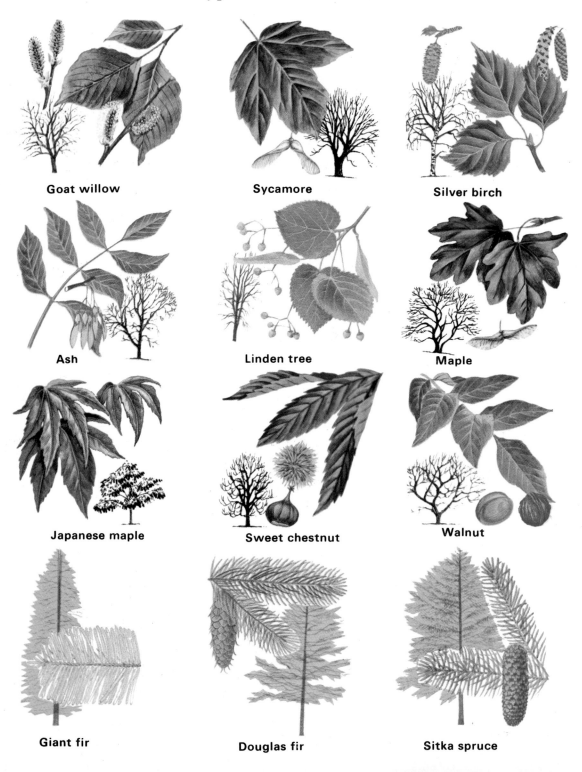

Goat willow

Sycamore

Silver birch

Ash

Linden tree

Maple

Japanese maple

Sweet chestnut

Walnut

Giant fir

Douglas fir

Sitka spruce

Lawson cypress

Wellingtonia

Lombardy poplar

White poplar

Deodar

Purple beech

Beech

London plane

Tulip tree

Spanish fir

Yew

Cycad

Lodgepole pine

Western pine

Larch

Domestic Animals

Animals which are tamed and used by man are called domestic animals. The dog was probably the first domestic animal. Even in the Bronze Age people tamed dogs to help them hunt. Then men began to tame other wild animals for their meat and skins and for their milk and wool. Soon farmers found that by choosing the best and fattest of their animals they could breed lots more fat, strong animals. They could get more meat and more milk. Farmers have been carefully breeding their best animals for hundreds of years. Today domestic animals look very different from their wild ancestors.

As well as giving men food and clothing, animals have been trained for many other uses. In some countries, oxen and buffalo are still used to plough the land. In Burma, elephants are used to carry heavy logs from the teak forests. In deserts, the camel has been used to carry people and their goods for thousands of years.

Wild pigs still live in some parts of the world. You can see how different the domestic pig is. It has been bred for its meat for two thousand years

Water buffalo are still used for ploughing the rice fields in many parts of Asia

Boxer

Toy poodle

Kerry blue terrier

Bloodhound

Pets

Man has not only tamed animals that are useful. Many dogs are trained to look after sheep, to help the police and to guard people, but most dogs are kept as pets. They make very good friends.

All pets must be well cared for. They must be properly fed and cleaned and allowed exercise. Cats are easy pets to keep. They do not have to be taken for walks and they clean themselves. Parrots and other cage birds are great fun. Some even learn to 'talk'. Rabbits, mice and hamsters can be kept in hutches in the garden. In winter tortoises dig a hole and go to sleep. They must never be woken up because it could kill them.

Studying Nature

People who study nature are called naturalists. They need to be very patient because wild animals are scared of people. They have to watch the animals without disturbing them. Sometimes they have to wait in 'hides' for hours before they see any animals. They watch how the animals stalk and hunt, eat and sleep, protect themselves and care for their young. They photograph the animals, record their voices and write notes about their habits.

Because so many animals are shy, naturalists often have to study them without seeing them. They study their nests and burrows and the tracks they make in the snow or mud. You can tell from an animal's footprints just what it was doing when it passed by.

Animal tracks.

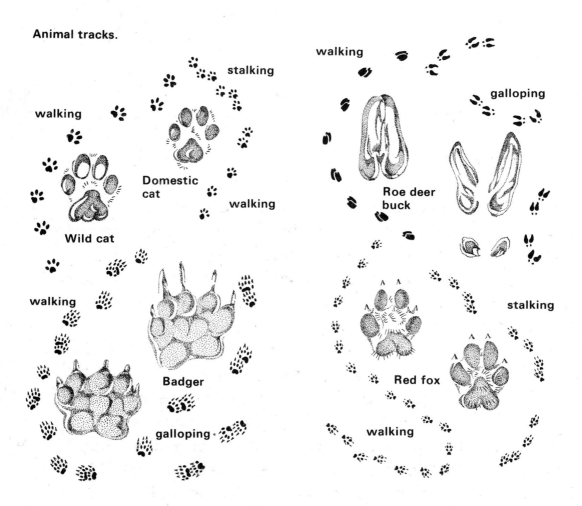

walking

stalking

galloping

walking

walking

Domestic
cat

Wild cat

Roe deer
buck

walking

stalking

Badger

Red fox

galloping

walking

178

A naturalist films the animals at a waterhole from his 'hide' in a tree.

Henri Fabre was a famous French naturalist who studied insects. He watched the ants and spiders crawling in his garden. He took walks in the countryside to observe dragonflies and bees. Everything he saw he wrote down to remember. Soon he came to know more about insects than any other person.

Charles Darwin travelled all around the world. He saw giant tortoises, a hundred years old, brightly coloured finches and strange lizards like small dragons. He took note of all their habits and saw how each different animal was fitted to the way it lived. Some of the finches had strong beaks like nutcrackers, good for opening hard seeds. The slow-moving tortoises were safe in their hard shells and some of the lizards could change colour and not be seen. Gradually Darwin realized why animals are all different and how modern animals came to be as they are. This discovery made him the world's most famous naturalist.

The Balance of Nature

Every plant and animal plays a part in the world of nature. And over the years the different plants and animals have become perfectly balanced. There are just enough plants, just enough plant-eating animals and just enough meat-eating animals. Sometimes too many meat-eating animals are born. Then they kill too many plant-eating animals. Some of the meat-eating animals starve to death and the balance is right again.

This balance of nature has been upset by man. Huge forests have been cut down for timber and land has been cleared for farming, houses and factories.

Thirsty Australian rabbits gather at a waterhole in the dry, dusty plain which they helped to cause.

A cheetah hunts down an antelope.
Both the hunter and the hunted play
a part in the web of nature.

More and more land is needed all the time and more and more animals are in danger as their homes are destroyed. Each year waste chemicals from factories are poured into rivers and lakes and the fishes and plants in them die. The foam from washing powders used in every home makes many rivers unfit for animals to live in. Sea birds and fishes are killed by oil dumped from ships. Other harmless creatures are killed by the chemicals sprayed on the land to kill pests. All the time animals and plants are being killed by carelessness.

Man has also upset the balance of nature by taking animals from one place to another. One hundred years ago a few rabbits were taken to Australia by a farmer and set free. The rabbits had no natural enemies in their new home and soon there were millions of them. They nibbled the grass down to its roots and turned large grasslands into dusty plains. Foxes and stoats were sent to Australia to feed on the rabbits. But the foxes and stoats found the Australian animals just as good to eat as rabbits. There are fewer rabbits in Australia now, but they will always be pests.

Conserving Nature

Many years ago millions of bison roamed the plains of America. And millions of zebras grazed on the African grasslands. Today the only herds of bison and zebra left are protected in large parks.

Many other animals are in great danger of becoming extinct. They have been killed for their skins and meat, shot by farmers and captured for zoos.

Many people are trying to keep, or conserve, the wild life which remains. National parks have been set up in many parts of the world where the animals can live in peace.

The Tasmanian wolf was hunted by farmers because it attacked their sheep. Now no one is sure if there are any Tasmanian wolves left alive

Pandas are very rare. There are only a few left in zoos and in the bamboo forests of China

The Auroch was a great ox that became extinct over three hundred years ago. It was hunted by man and its horns were used as drinking cups

There are not many orangs left in the wild but they are being bred in zoos

Most of the world's wild animals can be seen in zoos. For a long time zoos bought animals which had been captured in the wild. When the animals died the zoos simply bought some more. But as zoos became more and more popular, more and more animals were captured. Fewer and fewer were left in their natural homes. The orang-utan is a very popular animal in zoos. It is also quite easy to catch. So many orang-utans were caught and sold to zoos that there are not many left in the forests of Borneo where they live.

Today zoos breed many of their own animals. They also help to save very rare animals from becoming extinct. The Hawaiian goose is one animal which has been saved by zoos. Some years ago there were less than 20 Hawaiian geese left in the wild. Some were taken to a zoo and carefully bred. More and more geese were born. Now there are hundreds of these birds. Some have already been taken back to Hawaii and set free.

Index